Collins

need to know?

Dreams

Sean Callery

Collins

First published in 2006 by Collins
an imprint of
HarperCollins Publishers
77–85 Fulham Palace Road
London W6 8JB

www.collins.co.uk

09   08   07   06
5   4   3   2   1

A catalogue record for this book is available from
the British Library

Editor: Emma Callery
Designer: Bob Vickers
Series design: Mark Thomson
Front cover photograph: © Tom Stewart/CORBIS
Back cover photographs from top to bottom: Brand X
Pictures/Alamy; Westend61/Alamy; Banana
Stock/Alamy; Royalty-free/Corbis/
ImagineThat/Alamy

ISBN-13 978-0-00-721083-1
ISBN-10 0-00-721083-3

Colour reproduction by Colourscan, Singapore
Printed and bound by Printing Express Ltd,
Hong Kong

Contents

Introduction

People have been dreaming since the first humans lay down to sleep. They have been puzzling over their dreams for just as long – some of the earliest writings are about the subject. Interpreting dreams has long been part of our culture and people continue to wonder why we dream and what our dreams tell us.

must know

Common dreams
The following are common dream themes, which all of us are likely to experience some time, partly because they are widely held fears linked with everyday situations.
Monsters (see page 48)
Teeth (see page 63)
Being chased (see page 71)
Falling (see page 73)
Nudity (see page 75)
Taking a test (see page 78)
Paralysis (see page 83)
Death of friends or family (see page 129)
Relationships (including sex) with known or unknown people, especially celebrities (see People section on pages 148-63)
Flying (see page 175)

Messages from the gods

Many ancient cultures valued dreams as a source of knowledge and a time of contact with their gods. This idea that dreams were instances of divine communication led to the first dream interpreters becoming the first priests. Knowledge is power, and the perceived ability to understand your own and others' dreams brought power and status. It took centuries for religions to shake off their associations with dreams and visions and decide that their God communicated through scriptures, rather than dreams.

Dream interpretation subsequently became largely pagan, or at least non-religious, and dreams were seen as a source of omens. Today, there are millions of people around the world who believe that dreams can carry prophecies. Perhaps this fulfils a human need for security about the future just as astrology, tarot cards and other predictive practices do. Certainly the many websites devoted to dream interpretation frequently suggest that our dreams are predictive.

Research by many thinkers in the nineteenth century, culminating in the theories expounded by

Freud and Jung, brought the study of dreams a new legitimacy. They argued that dreams are the creations of our own minds, and reveal our innermost thoughts. If we understand our dreams, we learn more about ourselves. Furthermore, the very mind that created the dream can be employed to decode it.

Some psychologists believe dreams are part of our development and growth. Others disagree, suggesting that they are a mechanism for clearing out the memory so it does not get cluttered up with irrelevant information.

This book provides background on the cultural history of dreaming around the world, the development of modern dream theories, and provides a comprehensive guide to the symbolism we see in dreams, which reflects the symbolism of our world.

When considering your own dreams, remember:

▶ **Your mind made the dream,** so it should be able to unravel it.

▶ **Your symbolism may be different** to that of others. Use the dream diary to gain understanding of this (see pages 94–112).

▶ **Context is everything.** Try not to pick out individual symbols, but consider them as part of the overall story of your dream.

As the Greek philosopher Aristotle said thousands of years go: 'Dreaming is thinking while asleep.' Enjoy your thinking. Just don't do too much of it when you are trying to get to sleep!

1 Dream culture through history

The story of dream culture through the ages is a fascinating tale of our need to understand our world, the way our beliefs are shaped and, more recently, our efforts to understand how the human mind works.

Africa and the Middle East

These areas where humans first walked the earth are the place where people first dreamed, then pondered what a dream was and shared their dreams with their fellow beings. The Christian and Islamic religions were born in the Middle East, and both of them owe part of their story to dream interpretation.

must know

Egyptian meanings

Some Egyptian dream interpretations are clearly literal: for example, seeing yourself with your face to the ground means the dead (in the underworld) want something from you. Others use opposites, such as:

▶ **Falling** suggests prosperity.

▶ **Seeing yourself dead** means you'll have a long life.

Another type relies on word play. For instance, since the Egyptian word for 'buttocks' was similar to that for 'orphan', a dream where your buttocks are revealed is a forecast of the death of your parents.

Egypt

Ancient Egyptians believed that their many gods either shaped or took part in human dreams, which foretold the future. Since priests provided the link between mortals and the gods, they would interpret these divinely inspired dreams. Anyone who has seen an Egyptian temple will know that symbolism was second nature to the ancient Egyptians, and so they were very conversant with the idea of interpreting pictures and images.

To help them, papyrus dream books were created, possibly as early as the eighteenth century BC. One survives – known as the *Chester Beatty Papyrus* – and it gives details from more than a hundred dreams, which it classifies as being either 'good' or 'bad'. However, Egyptian dream diaries suggest that they also classified dreams into three main types, which were:

▶ **Dreams where gods** demanded action. An example is the god Harmarkis telling a young man that if he dug out the famous Sphinx in Cairo from its sand and re-built Hamarkis's temple, he would become pharaoh. He did so, and subsequently became the Pharaoh Tuthmosis IV. A plaque erected in 1400 BC between the Sphinx's paws tells the story.

▶ **Dreams foretelling** the future or giving the location of hidden treasures.

▶ **Dreams offering advice**, such as the best place to build a tomb.

Christianity and dreaming

Early Christians believed that God contacted them in dreams. Sometimes this would be in the form of a vision. *Joel* 2:28 states: 'I will pour out my spirit upon all flesh, and your sons and your daughters shall prophesy, your old men shall dream dreams, your young men shall see visions.' Visions might be seen in the daytime, sometimes induced by fasting, and therefore are not identified with sleep in the way that dreams are. Since dreams or visions involved messages from God, the first holy men were also dream interpreters.

The Old Testament of the Bible, and other Christian writings by those such as St Augustine and St John Chrysostom, are littered with references to dreams. Biblical figures such as Solomon, Jacob, Nebuchadnezzar and Joseph all received guidance from God or His prophets through their dreams. In the *Book of Genesis*, Jacob wrestles with an angel in a dream and is rewarded with his new name, Israel, and told he will start a new nation. *Exodus* records the story of his son, Joseph, who gained the favour of the pharaoh by telling him the meaning of his dreams. An example (quoted in *Genesis*) is a dream of seven lean cattle eating an equal number of fat cattle, which Joseph suggested prophesied seven years of plenty followed by seven years of famine.

As always, interpretation is all: one interesting note on the famous story of Abraham being told in a dream to sacrifice his son Isaac is that some interpreters feel he made a mistake and that the ram that he saw in his dream represented himself, and not his son.

Since God was communicating through dreams, the dreamer could not be held responsible for what he had seen. Anyone could meet God in this way, but might need to talk to a dream interpreter to discover its meaning. Incidentally, there is no mention of contact with dead people through dreams in the Bible (see also the box on trees and the Bible on page 147).

However, this view of dreams as a connection with God changed. The New Testament hardly mentions them, and they seem to have become identified with pagan, rather than Christian practice. When, in the fourth century, St Jerome declared that the dreams that tortured him were the work of the Devil, the new view was taken up with a vengeance. Dreams were no longer regarded as divine messages, because God communicated through the scriptures. Joan of Arc was burned at the stake because she would not be swayed in her belief that the visions she saw in dreams came from God (see also page 131).

Islam and dreams

Although Islam is a worldwide religion, its origins are in the Middle East, which is why it is included here.

Islam values dreams more highly than other religions. This may be partly because of the tradition that the prophet Muhammed received his first message from the angel Gabriel in a dream. The sacred text that Muhammed then wrote features many stories involving dreams, and advises that Muslims should sleep on their right side to help them to sleep and dream well. After his death, the Prophet is said to have appeared in the dreams of many caliphs. Muslim tradition has it that dreams are one forty-sixth prophecy.

Islamic dream visions

In the eleventh century, Abu Hamid al-Ghazali, wrote how non-prophets can achieve visions. He believed that dream visions came from the 'world of the angelic kingdom' where man goes when he dies. Those of good faith, with pure souls, would be able to see visions of this kingdom while they were still alive. We can only do this when we are asleep because then the senses are dormant and do not distract the dreamer. Upon wakening, the dreamer will only recall the images he has seen, which then need to be interpreted.

Islamic dream interpreting

In common with Arab culture, dreams are regarded as a time when inner, subtle senses are active and we are receptive to new ideas and spiritual inspiration. Help is needed to uncover the truths thus suggested. A famous early dream interpreter was Ibn Sirin, who died in AD 738. He always considered the character of the dreamer when interpreting dreams. Famously, two men who came to him within an hour of each other having both dreamed of being the caller to prayer were given utterly different interpretations. One, of good character, was to go on the pilgrimage to Mecca. The other, a rogue, was told he would be accused of theft.

The Americas

Dreams were (and are) an important part of Amerindian culture, but the practices and beliefs varied widely across the land. Some societies attached such importance to dreams that their language had special verb forms to show the action occurred in a dream.

did you know?

Dream catchers
North American tribes had many stories and legends about a spider that protected them from bad dreams. In some, the spider acts after a human saves its life. In others, it is a god-like giver of wisdom. What the stories share is the idea that a web can be woven that will allow good dreams to slide through its centre and flow down a feather to the dreamer. Bad dreams will be trapped in the web, where they will be destroyed at first light. A tradition developed of protecting the young and vulnerable by weaving such a dream catcher, and hanging it over the cradleboard on a piece of wood. Dream catchers are still given as gifts to children and newborn babies. The idea of spider webs offering protection may have evolved from the practice of covering wounds with them – apparently the web stems bleeding.

Knowledge from dreams

Dreams were an accepted part of life: they gave information on where to hunt or where to find food. It was accepted that the local medicine man would learn some of his treatments and medicines through his dreams.

In some native American cultures, spider webs are used to stem bleeding of open wounds. This protection is used symbolically through web designs on cots and blankets to stop children having bad dreams – which are believed to be capable of causing illness and even death (see left).

One practice common to many Amerindians in the past was fasting to induce sacred dreams. This seems to have been part of the induction of the young into the adult world, and involved helping them to make choices about the life they would lead in the future. The value of patience was indicated by a dream in which a bird (a culturally important symbol on this continent) offers riches for the future, but once rejected, is revealed to be a very small bird clearly lacking the powers it claimed.

Throughout native North America, dreaming and discussions contributed to a complex culture. Dreamers took pride in retelling their dreams, partly because the best way to stop unpleasant prophesies coming true was to share them with others. Dreams often involved contact with gods, animals or spirits. An element among Plains Indian cultures was the idea of visions during which someone in the dream offered a gift of special powers.

South American dream culture was similarly complex and varied. The Aguaruna people of Peru gathered for highly stylized 'dream declarations' in which they described and performed their dreams. The events were told in rhythmic chants, sometimes taking on the voices of the characters in the dream. The Raramuri in Mexico believed we have more than one soul and that in dreams one of these souls exits the body, and meets other souls. Others believe that we dream when our souls sleep.

In Chile and Guatemala the meaning of dreams was related more to events in the real world. So a dream would be interpreted differently according to the health of the dreamer or people in their family, or political events, earthquakes, trading deals and so on.

The spirit state

Dreams have long had an especially important role in Brazilian culture. One native writer described them as 'the moments in which we are stripped of the nanderekó, the rational structure of thought.' This allowed dreamers to achieve a pure state of spirit where they connect with a deeper reality and even to send their spirit on journeys during dreams. To the Brazilian Xavante people, dreaming remained a complex social action which, while allowing conversations with the dead, also contributed to the telling and retelling of myths, the sharing of ideas, and reinforcing the beliefs and rituals of their own community. Adolescent boys watched their ancestors in dreams, and told of their experiences in songs. Later they learnt to get so close to their ancestors that they became them in their dream. This idea of dreams becoming part of your identity and helping to shape your personality, is still widely followed in Brazil.

must know

The Iroquois American Indians

In this culture, it was felt that dreams showed our unconscious desires, and that these repressed wishes had to be acted out to keep the dreamer sane and healthy. When acting out the dream, social and moral barriers were ignored, so the dreamer could take another's property or even sleep with another's spouse. So dreams were part of a system that recognized and allowed the release of tensions to maintain social order.

Asia

Asia is home to the earliest recordings of dreams, made on clay tablets by the Sumerians of Mesopotamia in about 3100BC. Dream interpretation is still part of many people's lives across the whole continent.

Chinese dream temples
The Chinese built dream temples where dreams could be instigated. In the sixteenth century, a high official visiting a city would report to a temple on the first night to receive guidance for his mission. Judges and government officials were also expected to attend dream temples for advice.

Prophetic dreams

In the seventh century BC King Assurbanipal wrote of a dream shared by soldiers in his army in which the goddess Ishtar told them it was safe to cross the dangerously fast-flowing River Idid'e. This shows that dreams were regarded as prophetic. Assurbinipal also records that the goddess stated that she had created him to be king, handily supporting his right to rule!

Mesopotamians believed that their souls could travel when they were asleep, sometimes being carried by a god. This could be encouraged by spending the night in a room in that god's temple – an early instance of incubation (see page 21), which was also practised by the Greeks.

China

Interpreting dreams has been central to Chinese culture for thousands of years. The way in which dreams were viewed altered with the times, but they were taken very seriously.

Confucian dream interpretation
The earliest history of China, the *Zuo Zhuan* (attributed to Confucius and thought to date from the fourth or fifth century BC), paints dreams as a

timeless place where people from the past come into the present, often prophesying the future. Dead ancestors frequently appear in dreams to offer advice or thanks. An example is the story of Wei Ko, who followed his dying father's instructions that his concubine be allowed to marry after his death, despite the sick man earlier saying she should be killed. The woman's father appeared to him in a dream and thanked him for his decision.

The Chinese at this time saw shared dreams as proof of their truth. One example is when a minister called Xux Yan dreamed that after he had his head cut off by an opponent, he picked it up and ran. A shaman who shared the dream told him that it meant he would indeed die, but that his military expedition would succeed. The prophesy came true.

Some Chinese at this time linked dreams with the existence of spirits who become angry and enter the human world. A minister called Zichan ordered sacrifices to be made to appease the spirit of Gun, who controlled floods. Gun had appeared in the threatening form of a yellow bear entering the bedroom of the sick local ruler. The ruler recovered once the sacrifices were complete. Zichan explained: 'I provide the ghost with a place to return to.'

Chinese dream decoders were capable of showing admirable imagination in finding positives out of apparent negatives. Before a battle in 632 BC with the Chu ruler, Duke Wen of Jin dreamed that his enemy pushed him to the ground and sucked out his brain, and was understandably terrified. His minister took the opposite view: 'Our side received heaven, while Chu bent down as if accepting

did you know?

Dream court ruling
A courtroom drama shows the status of dreams in Chinese society. A woodcutter from Zheng killed and hid a deer, but then forgot where he had put it and decided it had been a dream. When he told the story, another man followed his directions, and found the animal. His wife suggested (rather cunningly, you might think) that he might have dreamed the conversation with the woodcutter. There was then, of course, an almighty argument about who owned the deer. The case went to court, where the judge told them to share the animal as they could both have dreamt some of the events.

must know

The source of dreams
Vedic scriptures describe three states: the jagrata (awakened state), svapna (dreaming state) and susupti (deep sleep). They suggest that our dreams are created by either:
▶ **Krishna**, the supersoul, who can use them to deliver omens or
▶ **Ghosts**, whose dreams seem to be more negative.

punishment.' He also argued that the brain would have softened Chu's teeth, thus showing that their opponent was in fact weakened. Jin went on to win the battle.

Chinese dream philosophy

Chinese dream interpretation changed about a century after the *Zuo Zhuan*, with the Taoist work *Zhuangzi*. This viewed dreams in a more philosophical way, as being about achieving a higher consciousness. By this stage, the Chinese seemed to be more interested in the process of dreaming than the content of the dreams. Dreams were also about transformation. For example, a famous dream in which Zhuang Gzi was a carefree butterfly plays with the idea of his identity when he woke up. Was he still the butterfly, dreaming he was a man? How do we know if we really exist? It is a philosophical question that man has pondered for centuries (as in Descartes' famous statement 'I think therefore I am'). Dreams therefore helped the ancient Chinese to see humans as transitory beings on a journey through life, and thus reconcile them to death.

India

There is a long history of dream study in the Indian subcontinent. The sacred books of the Veda, written between 1500 and 1000 BC, set out the basic beliefs of the Ayurveda, an ancient Indian medical approach that links health with control over your way of life. The Veda (which is the basis of Hinduism) includes a section that categorizes dreams according to whether they are favourable or not. Ayurveda divides people in terms of the combination of elements (earth, fire, air and water) of their personality, further grouping them according to their nature and body type. Ayurvedic doctors believe that people of certain types have certain dreams. For example, someone linked to the elements of water and earth is more likely to see water in dreams, and water-related birds and flowers, such as lotuses.

A set of texts expanding on the Veda, called the *Upanishads*, offers two contrasting views on dream interpretation:
- ▶ **Dreams express our inner desires.**
- ▶ **The soul leaves the body** during dreaming. If the dreamer is suddenly awakened, the soul might be unable to return and the sleeper might die.

The Sufi religion
Dream interpretation was an important element in the Sufi religion from its earliest times. For example, Baha ad-din Naqshband of Bukhara (d. 1389), after whom the Naqshbandi Order of Sufism is named, was well known as an interpreter of dreams and only accepted some visitors if he was shown their suitability in a dream.

The influence continues, for Hazrat Inayat Khan, an Indian Sufi teacher who started The Sufi Order in the West (now called the Sufi Order International) in the early part of the twentieth century, wrote extensively about dreams. He believed they enhance our understanding of ourselves and of the world by giving a voice to our own imagination. He felt every dream had meaning, sometimes symbolic, at other times a vision of the past or the future.

Aboriginal dreamtime
The widely known link between Aboriginal people and dreamtime is a source of some confusion when studying dream meaning. In this context, 'dreamtime' is a general term for these native people's history, wisdom, morality and spirituality, in particular the idea that the past, present and future exist together. It does not relate directly and only to dreams as we refer to them. However, many of the 500-plus tribal groups believe that there is interaction between the dead and the living in dreams, something they share with many ancient cultures.

Europe

The ancient civilizations of Europe esteemed dreams as much as others around the globe. However, Europe was the scene for the shift in dream interpretation from being a religious to an essentially pagan activity. Modern dream theory also began to evolve on this continent.

must know

True or false?
The Ancient Greeks believed the Gods might choose to send 'true' or 'false' dreams and they tried to distinguish between them. This was done by deciding if the dream came through a particular gate.

▶ **False, meaningless dreams** came through a sawn ivory gate.
▶ **True dreams** came through a polished horn gate.
Odysseus and Penelope discuss the difference in Homer's *Iliad*.

Ancient Greece

The Ancient Greeks believed they received messages from the gods in their dreams, which could only be interpreted by their priests. Homer's *Iliad*, dating from the eighth century BC, features King Agamemnon being given instructions by a messenger of Zeus. Greek gods were believed to use dreams to punish those who angered them, and the king was one such victim. He had stolen a slave girl from the warrior Achilles, and Zeus sent a messenger to tell him to march on Troy as he was guaranteed victory. When the king's troops followed his orders, his army was defeated.

At first it was just Zeus, King of the Gods, who sent divine dreams, but later other gods, such as Athena, Hera, Artemis, Asklepios, Hermes and Pan (the 'conductor of dreams'), were believed to be involved. Two gods in particular became important to dreamers: Hypnos ruled sleep while his son, Morpheus, ruled dreams. The healing cult of Asclepius shows the great value placed on these divine communications.

The cult of Asclepius survived for seven centuries in Ancient Greece. It set up a series of temples that sound rather like our modern disorder treatment centres where people go to forget their troubles and sometimes seek advice on addiction.

Born of the god Apollo and a mortal mother (who Apollo then killed in a fit of jealousy, rescuing his son from her body on its funeral pyre), Asclepius became a healer. After the King of the Gods, Zeus, finished him off with a thunderbolt for daring to bring the dead back to life, Asclepius was worshipped as the god of healing. The sick would visit sanctuaries called Asclepions (the most famous was at Epidaurus), taking with them offerings such as sacrificial animals or small, flat, honey cakes. They were given treatment, and avoided 'impure' foods such as alcohol. Then they went to an incubation room where, it was hoped, the god would visit them in a dream, sometimes as a dog or snake. The room was supposed to induce a magic dream, which would either heal them outright, or tell them how to cure themselves.

One story that survives is that of Ambrosia of Athens, who was blind in one eye. She mocked the suggested cures for the lame and blind, yet in her sleep Asclepius cut her eyeball and poured in medicine. He told her to dedicate a silver pig in the temple as an offering in memory of her ignorance. When she woke, she could see. The story is significant because, unusually for Greek texts, it refers to a woman's dream. Women were especially likely to go to Asclepius for guidance to do with pregnancy and childbirth.

Who creates dreams?

Philosophers would debate whether there was any truth in the divination of meaning from dreams, especially the idea that they came from outside forces such as gods. In the fifth century BC, the extremely influential philosopher Heraclitus of Ephesus put forward the idea that dreams were created by the minds of people. Aristotle (384–322 BC) developed this idea in his rational study of the dreaming process, and was convinced there was a connection between dreams and bodily health.

Grecian belief in the power of dreams survived their empire's later amalgamation into the Roman empire, for it is then that we meet Artemidorus of Ephasus (AD 150–200), who lived in Roman Asia (now Turkey). One of many professional dream interpreters, he produced five volumes of a work called *Oneirocritica* (*The Interpretation of Dreams*), the earliest known book on dream meaning. It draws on other (undiscovered) texts on dreams to suggest there are two classes of dreams:

▶ **Future-forecasting** – '**somnium**' – and
▶ '**Insomnium**', which were allegorical dreams influenced by the dreamer's state of body and mind.

In order to decide the meaning of this second group of dreams, Artemidorus felt it was vital to talk to the dreamer about his life, health, personality and typical dream images. This suggests that he was using therapy as a means of diagnosis, and derived symbolic meanings from the dreams reported. Such was his influence that the *Oneirocritica* was reproduced in Byzantine, Arabic and Latin forms as late as the eighteenth century.

Artemidorus saw each dream as unique once he had considered the personality of the dreamer. Some dream symbols were universal, but others could change. An example is the dove, a symbol of Christian peace and hope, but also a bird blessing from Aphrodite. The meaning depended on the dreamer's own history – an idea that was revived in the late nineteenth century as psychologists began to take dreams seriously as an indicator of mental wellbeing.

Roman dreams

The Romans were for a time very enthusiastic dream interpreters, drawing on the culture of the Greeks and the Egyptians. It is even said that the emperor Augustus proclaimed that any dreams that included prophesies about the future of the Roman state should be proclaimed at the forum, to ensure all were kept informed. The Roman gods who became linked with dreams were Fauna (or Bona Dea), for women, and her brother (or husband) Faunus, for men.

As the influence of Christianity took hold, however, such practices were labelled as pagan and were not encouraged by the Roman government. Officially, there was plenty of divination using other methods, but no dream oracles. However, the belief persisted and, in private, Roman citizens continued to shell out plenty of denarii to specialists to interpret their dreams.

Dreaming in the Middle Ages

People were fascinated by dreams in the Middle Ages in the West. Many books were published describing the dreams of the rich, powerful and faithful, and a new trend emerged of autobiographical writings including the writer's dreams. At the same time, women's dreams were reported more widely than in earlier texts from Egypt and Greece. New books of classification of types of dream and dream symbols were written and widely discussed.

With religion so closely linked to the running of the state, it became common for those who sought religious advancement to quote support from saints and clerical figures in revelations they had seen in dreams.

There was a fear that both God and the Devil could influence dreams, and the fact that dreams happen in the dark, when we lie dormant and close to the state of death, supported the fear that this was when we were more receptive to evil thoughts. So the powerful clergy became much more positive about visions,

must know

Nostradamus
The famous Michel
Nostradamus (1503–1566),
whose writings allegedly predict
events such as the rise to power
of Hitler and the assassination of
John F. Kennedy, also took great
interest in dreams. He wrote
an A–Z of dream interpretation
and offered interpretations of
common dreams, all in his
distinctive quatrain style. Some
of his interpretations are given in
the box opposite.

which were considered more likely to come from God, as they usually occurred in the daytime. To have visions when you were awake was to show moral worth and saintliness.

Hebrews continued to see dreams as pictures from God, which could therefore be interpreted. They were seen as a way to encourage the faith of the dreamer. In medieval times, rabbis began to issue books aiding dream interpretation.

However, there was now an uneasy divide between those who accepted that dreams could be messages from God, and those who felt he only communicated through the scriptures and therefore dream interpretation was a relic from pagan times or, worse, the work of the Devil. In the Reformation, the view of dreams as diabolic work was cemented, as exemplified by the founder of Protestantism, Martin Luther, saying sin was 'the confederate and father of foul dreams'.

Dream guides

With the invention of the printing press and therefore the wider distribution of books, many titles were published offering interpretations of dreams, indicating it was a subject of wide interest. Here's a tour through the early part of the alphabet of dream symbols from the seventeenth to the nineteenth centuries:

Adders (1695)

'To fight with adders signifies the overthrow of enemies.' Snakes continue to be a symbol of evil (see page 50).

Banquet (1750)

'To dream that you are at banquets and do not eat, denotes shortage of money,' so dreaming of being poor means you are poor. Similarly, from a different book published in the same year: 'To dream you have fat cheeks is good; if thin, bad.'

Ball (1830)

'To dream you see persons dance at a ball, or that you are at a ball yourself signifies joy, pleasure, recreation or inheritance.'

Cage (1830)

'To dream that a girl lets a bird out of a cage is a sign that she will not keep her virginity, but as soon as she can will part with her maidenhead.' Birds remain for some a symbol of innocence.

Burning (1850)

'To dream you see burning lights descending from heaven is a very bad sign indeed and portends some dreadful accident to the dreamer.' So fire was not a good omen, but then neither was water in 1870: 'To dream of an admiral denotes loss of trade; to see one in a naval engagement signifies that you will meet your death by drowning.'

must know

Nostradamus's dream interpretations

▶ **Keys:** *To dream your keys are gone or lost/Shows that you'll soon be vexed or crossed*
▶ **Cherries:** *To dream of cherries doth declare/That thou wilt many pleasures share/But from excess thou must refrain/Or e'en your pleasures will bring pain*
▶ **Death:** *To dream of death a marriage means/So variegated are life's scenes*

The first two of these interpretations can be read as simple injunctions to take care of possessions and to eat wisely, but the third is more interesting, for the idea of death as a symbol for rebirth is still argued by some dream interpreters.

Changing meanings

While some of these meanings are simply baffling to us now, they make more sense given a cultural context. For example, someone with lots of sheep in 1695 would have been rich and of high status, so dreaming of them 'signifies wealth and plenty' according to a book of that year. Nowadays we identify sheep with their lack of independence and would see sheep as a negative, passive metaphor. However, as has been noted, some interpretations still have echoes in how we analyse our dreams today. They also indicate the popularity of the idea that dreams were prophecies, and a complete lack of consideration of the relevance of the dream to the life and experiences of the dreamer in their waking life. As is shown on pages 26-9, the idea that dreams come from our own subconscious and therefore reflect our inner selves was not to emerge until the nineteenth century.

Modern dream analysis

In the nineteenth century, scientists were increasingly interested in the workings of the human mind, and this led them to study dreams. There was a resulting deeper understanding of what triggers dreams and their contents, after centuries of dream interpretation being written off as a kind of sorcery.

Early foundations

Nineteenth-century French doctor Alfred Maury studied 3,000 dreams and kept his own dream diary. A dream in which he was to be guillotined and awakened to find that the top of his bed had landed on him just at the point of impact with the blade in his dream led him to the theory that dreams are influenced by what is happening around us as we sleep. He experimented with various external stimuli, like scent on his pillow. His work echoed the suggestion by Aristotle over 2,000 years previously that dreams reflect what is happening to and in our bodies.

In the late part of the nineteenth century, scientists discovered that:

▶ **Dreams incorporate recent memories**, especially of the previous day.

▶ **Dreams can draw on** long forgotten memories and experiences.

▶ **Dream content** can be influenced by word play (so being in a dark room might suggest you feel you are being 'kept in the dark' about something).

▶ **In dreams we think in pictures.**

▶ **We have fewer inhibitions** in our dreams (so we can murder, or break with social norms), and thus reveal more of our basic nature.

While many researchers could find no useful role for dreams, the idea that they released repressed tensions began to gain acceptance. Thus were the foundations laid for the theories of Sigmund Freud (1856–1939).

Freudian theory

A doctor and neurologist, Freud became interested in the developing field of psychology and how dreams could show the inner workings of the mind. At first, he believed that dreams allowed the dreamer to act out their fantasies – a dream was merely pleasurable wish fulfilment. However, this theory does not explain the common experience of having nightmares or recurrent frightening dreams.

The next stage was his development of the three-part division of the human personality:

▶ **The id,** our animal urges and instincts – our selfish demand for gratification.

▶ **The superego,** which is our moral and ethical conscience and tries to block out the id.

▶ **The ego,** the rational, conscious mind, which balances the other two elements. In effect, Freud had discovered our subconscious.

The id's messages are altered to more acceptable images by the superego so the dream becomes a battleground between the ego and superego. This contest disguises the meanings of our dreams, which now require interpretation for us to enhance our self-knowledge.

Underlying all this was Freud's conviction that sexuality influences all our thoughts, and that most dreams are about sex and/or unresolved emotions from our childhood. This is concealed by the fact that images in dreams are symbolic, but, Freud argued, these symbols have a consistent meaning for all of us – for example, towers, spires and pencils are all phallic. He divined the meanings of these symbols by a technique known as 'free association', where new meanings are found for dream images by exploring the subconscious mind.

Freud was the first person to make a clear connection between our desires and our dreams, and to help the patient to make sense of them. Freud waited until 1900 to publish his *Interpretation of Dreams* so that it appeared symbolically at the start of a new century. His views divided his contemporaries, but someone who initially accepted his ideas with enthusiasm and then later questioned them and created a new theory of dream interpretation was Carl Jung (1875–1961).

Jungian archetypes
Jung argued that a number of key figures and symbols inhabit our collective unconscious, emerging in our dreams. Known as archetypes, each represents different aspects of the psyche, through which the dreamer can gain self-knowledge and can therefore progress towards maturity. These archetypes are drawn from myths, fairy tales and religions, and form part of a culture shared around the world. An archetype embodies the characteristics and behaviours identified with its figure. Each has its own entry in the book:
Anima (see page 156)
Animus (see page 156)
Divine Child (see page 152)
Great Mother (see page 158)
Father (see page 153)
Hero (see page 155)
Old Man/Woman (see page 160)
Shadow Stranger (see page 161)
Trickster (see page 162)
Non-human archetypes include the sun, moon, stars, rivers, fires and animals. These are also included in this book.

Jungian theory

Carl Jung (1875–1961) studied and used Freud's theories for many years. However, he found Freud's rigid views on the nature of dreams, their link with our past, and their symbolism too restricting. An example is his rejection of Freud's interpretation of his house dream (see page 119). Instead, Jung developed his own theories, based on the following concepts:

▶ **The ego** is our own sense of self.

▶ **It has a kind of shadow,** called the counter-ego, which supports opposite traits (such as the feminine aspects of a masculine man).

▶ **In addition to our conscious ego,** we have an unconscious one. This is a set of personal and cultural references, many of them common to plenty of other people, and known as the collective unconscious. It is not dominated by ideas of sexuality, but rather by ancient myths and archetypes (see box to the left).

▶ **Dreams are the meeting place** for the conscious and unconscious egos.

▶ **Thus, dreams are not hidden messages** about our past, but they reveal our thoughts about the present.

▶ **Symbolism** can be personal to each of us, and can be divined by 'direct association' where the mind is concentrated on the image.

▶ **We can learn from ourselves** by considering a number of dreams and identifying their themes.

The overall message of Jungian theory is more positive than that of Freud: we are essentially healthy, and exploring our dreams helps us to grow spiritually and as emotionally well-balanced people by acting as our own guide and adviser.

Evolving dream interpretation

Freud and Jung are the giants of modern dream interpretation, for they created the foundation for everything that followed. However, psychologists have continued to study dreams and contrasting theories have evolved. A few key stages include:

▶ **Alfred Adler** (1870–1937) stated that dreams have no hidden meanings, but simply illustrate our desire for personal growth. We dream to help solve problems, sometimes by identifying conflicting aspects of our own characters.

▶ **Medard Boss** (1903–1990) suggested that dreams simply reflect our lives and are not symbolic.

▶ **Calvin Hall** (1909–1985) analysed the contents of more than 50,000 dreams and revealed that:

  - Nearly a quarter of dreams were set in a house or building.
  - The dreamer was the sole character in 15% of dreams.
  - The other characters were strangers in more than four out of ten dreams, a slightly higher proportion than when they were friends or acquaintances.

▶ **Fritz Perls** (1893–1970) encouraged the dreamer to ponder how they unconsciously formed their dream, allowing them to gain insights into their own behaviour (this process is known as Gestalt therapy and can involve having a waking conversation with the dream character). So dreams are personal and there is no collective unconscious.

▶ **The idea of dreams using puns and word play** has a number of followers. For example, gilt can mean guilt.

▶ **Psychologist Bill Domhoff** believes he can develop a profile of a person's character if he is provided with information from about 70 of their dreams. His statistical analysis reveals that:

  - Men dream most about men, and show more aggression in dreams.
  - Half of children's dreams involve animals, compared to 5% of adults'.
  - A tenth of dreams include sex, hugs or kisses.

must know

Dream research today
Thousands of researchers (some of them dubbed 'oneironauts' from the Greek words for dreams (*oneiros*) and sailors (*nautos*) continue to study dreams in various ways. One ongoing debate is about whether we need to dream at all, with some analysts saying dreams are irrelevant, but that we do need to achieve REM (see page 32). Millions of people remain fascinated by the content of dreams – as shown by the huge number of websites devoted to dream interpretation and the popularity of books about them (see pages 184-5).

2 Managing dreams

The idea of managing dreams may seem strange to you, for, after all, when we are asleep we cannot control our thoughts – which is why we often dream things that are unpleasant or unwelcome. However, if we show interest in our dreams, we recognize their importance and make more of an effort to remember them. This, in turn, will influence what you dream about. The most advanced approach is to guide your own dreams, a process called lucid dreaming, covered on page 37.

What happens when we sleep?

It is very hard to get to sleep when you are worried about something, because your brain remains active. When we are wide awake, our brain pulsates up to 30 times a second. In the deepest, dreamless sleep, the rate can be as low as one a second.

must know

Sleepwalking
Sleepwalking, like night terrors, takes place in the deepest stage of non-REM sleep, when our muscles are not paralysed. It can be harmful because the dreamer is oblivious to danger. Help sleepwalkers by:
► Steering them gently back to bed – don't try to waken them.
► Fitting bars on upstairs windows.
► Putting up stair gates.
► Locking doors.

The sleep cycle

Once we fall asleep, we go into a five-stage cycle lasting about 90 minutes, so in an eight-hour sleep, this happens five times. The length of each stage varies.

► **Stage 1:** The pulse and breathing slow as the muscles relax. Temperature and blood pressure fall.

► **Stage 2:** The body continues to slow as we enter a light sleep.

► **Stage 3:** This is a deep, dreamless sleep during which time the immune system sets to work battling against disease. This is why we sleep more when we are ill.

► **Stage 4:** A very deep sleep during which the body regenerates.

► **Stage 5:** REM sleep.

REM sleep is a time of increased brain activity and **R**apid **E**ye **M**ovement. This is when we have our most vivid dreams, which are more likely to be remembered, especially if we wake up during them. It was discovered by chance during studies of sleeping babies in the 1950s.

Were you floating above yourself?
Stories of people feeling they left their body and watched themselves, or even travelled instantly to

other places, have been told for thousands of years. Out of body experiences (OBEs) generally take place at times of trauma-like near-death. Although technically not dreams, these changes in consciousness are so close to the dream state that they merit a mention in this book. As with predictive dreams, we may find it very hard to accept them as fact, but if anything, there is more evidence for these than of pre-cognition.

Types of dream

There are many kinds of dream.

▶ **Most deal with the events** of everyday life and are hardly worth recalling.

▶ **Some, on the other hand,** leave the dreamer with a sense of profound discovery (Jung categorized these as 'Great' dreams).

▶ **Others prompt an understanding** of a problem without the sense of revelation.

▶ **Another type** can be described as hallucinatory visions (which can occur to us at various times, including when we are awake, and can also be induced by drugs or starvation). These can involve powerful images that are disturbing and haunt the dreamer for some time.

▶ **Nightmares** are another type of dream that can be truly terrifying.

Recurring dreams

Recurring dreams are common. The same or similar event is repeated in dream after dream, and on average this continues for more than eight years. Given that dreams are created by our own minds, it is no surprise that similar themes and actions are repeated, just as there are echoes throughout our waking lives. However, recurring dreams are often unsettling, and since this type of dream is triggered by some behaviour trait or anxiety, the dream is likely to continue until you resolve the issue that is prompting it. So your priority should be to analyse the dream, discern the message from your subconscious, and try to deal with it. One variation of this type of dream is a serial dream, when the events change as circumstances alter (just as our perception of relationships changes over time). Again, the dream is a message telling you to address some underlying problem.

Telling the future

Many people believe dreams can foretell the future, and this idea has been accepted for thousands of years. Plenty of others mock the very idea that our fate is pre-ordained and, what's more, we receive clues about it in our dreams.

▶ **Psychic dreams** (also known as psi or anomalous dreams) are supposedly a manifestation of extrasensory perception (ESP), when information is given that we could not have obtained otherwise.

▶ **Pre-cognitive dreams** might be a prediction of the death of a relative, or some sense of connection with another person.

Whatever your views, it is worth noting that:

▶ **If we believe something will happen,** we are more likely to try to make it happen.

▶ **Many prophetic dreams** do not come true.

▶ **It is possible that our subconscious** is able to piece together bits of information and work out what is likely to happen next, which then appears as a prophetic dream.

▶ **Since we do not fully understand** how the brain works, such dreams could be a way of it communicating that we simply do not understand.

Nightmares

Every night, thousands of people wake up full of fear after a nightmare. Half of all adults have them occasionally (maybe just once a year) and about 1% have one a week. Children are far more likely to suffer them. The young (ages 3–12) have nightmares after they start to develop their own imagination – so it is a sign that they are growing healthily. At this age they are also beginning to discover the dangers and uncertainties of our lives and our world. Nightmares are unsettling for young children as they can be confused about whether what they experienced was real or not. Nightmares are more common during 'dreaming' or REM sleep.

Nightmares can be caused by anxiety about events during the day or more general concerns, for example, death or loneliness. They usually entail being chased or attacked. Equally disturbing can be a nightmare where the dreamer is behaving violently.

Remember that dreams are a way for us to come to terms with problems of safety and security, so a nightmare is not necessarily a bad thing: it may be a route to wellbeing. If you suffer nightmares, try to decide what is unsettling you. Some analysts argue that adults begin having nightmares when they have the emotional strength to deal with the issues and intense feelings involved – so, ironically, nightmares can be a sign of growing maturity: now you can deal with the problem.

The following gives advice on how to help children deal with and avoid nightmares. Many of these tips will be helpful to adults as well, but you should also read the next section on controlling your dreams. Persistent nightmares can be an indication of anxiety and depression.

Dealing with children's nightmares

If a child wakes up after a nightmare:

▶ Comfort him but don't go over the details of the dream if you can avoid it – you can do that in the morning when they will seem less scary.

▶ Reassure him that the dream is not real and encourage him to go back to sleep.

▶ If the child is having trouble settling, sit the other side of the door, calling out reassurance every five minutes until he falls asleep. You could stay in the room but this might set an inconvenient precedent!

▶ Be aware that the child might be frightened of going back to sleep, or of going to sleep the next day, in case the dream recurs. During the day, remind him that dreams are not real.

Next day:

▶ Invite your child to tell you the dream if he remembers it. He could draw what was frightening him, then symbolically throw away the image. Or he could act it out in order to explore how he could have escaped in the dream.

▶ If he can identify what was frightening him, tell him to pretend he has made it tiny enough to hold in his hand. Let him both ask it questions and suggest its response. This shrinks the threat so that it is not frightening.

▶ During a calm time, role-play what both of you will do if the child wakes from a nightmare. This is reassuring and gives you both a secure routine to follow when the time comes.

▶ Get him to suggest ways he would feel calmer and safer, and how he would like to get to sleep. This gives him 'ownership'.

▶ If the dreams persist, think about what could be prompting them. Is something causing the child stress? Keep a dream diary (see page 94) to see if there is a pattern, like the dream occurring on the same day, or after a certain meal.

Helping children avoid nightmares

▶ Don't use the bedroom as a place of punishment – it will have unhappy connotations at bedtime. If necessary, have a 'naughty step' or 'naughty room' elsewhere.

▶ The child's room should be quiet and dark (possibly with a comforting night-light).

▶ Avoid extremes of temperature and outside disturbance.

▶ Stick to a calm, clear routine (bath and story) at bedtime to relax your child. Avoid frightening stories or videos and lively play. Story tapes or familiar music might help.

▶ Allow your child to use a comforter like a blanket or a teddy. If possible, keep a spare or encourage him to choose from more than one to avoid crises.

▶ Keep bedtime at roughly the same time each evening, and don't allow napping during the day.

► Make it clear from the start that you expect your child to be able to go to sleep on his own, without you in the room.

► Don't allow heavy late meals, or excessive drinking. Forbid stimulating drinks in the hours up to bedtime.

► Use a dream pillow – see page 39.

Controlling your dreams

If you are often having bad dreams, or are simply baffled by or anxious about their content, you can learn to control them to a degree. You can do this by becoming aware during a dream that you are dreaming, and from that, directing the action. After all, the dream came from your own imagination in the first place! This is called lucid dreaming. In lucid dreams you can:

► Manipulate events.

► Confront threats and fears.

► Resolve nightmares.

In this way you can gain self-knowledge and hence build self-confidence. Some lucid dreamers even argue that in effect you prolong your life, because you continue your experiences while asleep!

How to learn lucid dreaming

Lucid dreaming is a skill, and like all skills, some people are more accomplished at it than others, but everyone can learn it to a degree.

Phase one: remember and record your dreams

This makes you more familiar with their content and keeps you 'in tune' with the idea of dreaming.

► **Keep a dream journal** (start by using the one bound into this book, see pages 97–112) by the bed, plus a pen or pencil and, if necessary, a torch.

► **As soon as you wake up,** whatever the time, spend a few seconds recalling the dream. How did it start? What was the structure? Try not to move or start thinking about the day ahead.

▶ **Then write it into your journal.** Dream memories seem to disappear faster than any others, and dialogue in particular fades rapidly, so start by recording what was said.

▶ **If writing the whole dream** seems like too much of a chore in the middle of the night, make notes. Record key details and feelings.

▶ **Train your memory by doing memory** exercises and playing memory games.

▶ **Read your dream diary** and look for patterns and themes. Is there anything you dream that has a special meaning for you?

Phase two: encouraging lucid dreams
Prompt this by asking yourself several times a day, 'Am I dreaming?' This encourages an automatic response, which will be useful in your dreams.

▶ **Get plenty of sleep.** If you are rested, you are more able to focus on your dream.

▶ **Sometimes a change of location prompts memorable dreams.** Try moving the bed to a different part of the room, or even sleeping at a friend's house.

▶ **Relax at bedtime.** Stick to a routine you are comfortable with, which could include yoga or relaxation exercises, reading, having a calming drink (see opposite).

▶ **Get in the habit of visualizing.** Sportspeople are among those who use this technique, whereby they mentally rehearse certain actions or thoughts. This process will help you control your dreams.

▶ **Some lucid dreamers** consciously build a two-hour break into their sleeping routine, because the sleep following the break (during which you simply relax, perhaps reading) produces more vivid dreams.

Phase three: controlling lucid dreams

Keep up the habit of asking 'Am I dreaming?' You can check if you are having a dream and are unaware of it by looking twice at the clock or a piece of writing. If you are dreaming, the time or the text will change. In ludcid dreams, eople can also suddenly look different.

▶ **Once you realize** you are 'inhabiting' a dream, don't start trying to control it. Treat it like an interactive television or game where you can adjust settings like light and where the camera is pointing.

▶ **Eventually you can train yourself** to control events. One analyst learned to extend his arm to pick up any object he could see without changing his position.

▶ **If you find yourself confronting** some demon or threat, resist the impulse to destroy it. It is a message from your subconscious that you need to understand, so study it.

▶ **Some dreamers** picture a 'dream mirror' so that they can study their dream surroundings without becoming consciously involved in moving, which can break up the dream.

Herb help

A dream pillow can help to encourage dreams, and even prompt certain kinds of dream. If your child is suffering from bad dreams, this may help. A dream pillow is just a muslin bag half filled with dried or fresh herbs (so it will flatten), which you place in your pillowcase. The heat from your head will stimulate the release of the scent. Follow your own personal taste to find a soothing, relaxing scent. Smell is actually our most evocative sense, so some fragrances may remind you of incidents in your life. Lavender is a very popular choice as it is so relaxing, but other possibilities are given above right.

3 Understanding dream symbols

The following sections offer suggestions for the meanings of what you see and sense in your dreams. The most likely source for an accurate interpretation will always be you: you created the dream, and it will reflect how your mind works and the associations it makes. However, the following guidance will prompt you to consider the metaphorical meaning of every aspect of your dream, and steer you towards possible meanings, because as human beings we share many cultural and everyday experiences, which shape our ideas and perceptions. Treat it as a set of prompt notes from which your own imagination (the source of your dream!) can lead you to greater understanding.

Animals and other creatures

Animals such as wolves, lambs, lions and foxes in children's tales recognizably have symbolic characteristics. Animals also represent ourselves at our most primitive, especially our sexuality. For ease of use, reptiles and sea creatures are included among the animals in this section.

Alligator

Alligators clearly represent a threat of some kind. You may fear something, possibly being overwhelmed by certain basic feelings or instincts. There may be a warning here that deception is taking place – so it could be a signal to re-evaluate a relationship, or advice on a business deal. Taming such a creature indicates feelings of power and competence. Because they are often half submerged, these animals reveal what is on the edge of our subconscious. Their large jaws suggest greed.

Ape

Apes symbolize wild and unpredictable behaviour, especially in social situations. This could be a warning about being deceived or made to look a fool. Dreams about large apes appearing in unusual places can indicate a fear of the unexpected. There may be an element of word play, with someone 'going ape' and needing to calm down.

Ass

An ass can be a good, simple, hardworking worker, but it can also be stubborn and uncooperative. Consider the context in your dream and your life. If you are the ass being ridden by someone else, you may be feeling undervalued and put-upon. If you are riding the ass, this can indicate feelings of social inadequacy. Falling off the animal shows lack of harmony and balance in relationships. Leading the animal shows feelings of control and a sense of direction. Of course, the other meaning of ass is a fool, so being chased by an ass suggests that someone is trying to make a fool out of you.

Bat

Bats tend to be seen as bad omens. Indeed, to the Australian Aborigines they are a symbol of death. We identify them with lack of cleanliness and a feeling of being out of control, so they may signal concerns about an argument, or a need to change behaviour (indicating there may be an element of needing to alter your ways here). Bats come out in the dark, which symbolizes our inner self, so the bat is carrying a message from your subconscious. (See also Vampire.)

Bear

Bears represent solitary aggression and bad temper. Taking the first element, this may be a sign of introspection and self-analysis. The second is clearly about feeling threatened, or having to compete and overcome obstacles. Bears kill, so there may be some thoughts of death, and possibly rebirth. To some Amerindians, the bear is a male authority figure possessing wisdom and sacred knowledge.

Bull

The bull is a symbol of fertility and strength, so there is a close link with sex drive and/or assertiveness here. If the bull is untamed, so, too may be your passions, and you may need to compromise in some way.

▶ **A pair of fighting bulls** suggests two warring brothers. Remember the phrase 'bull-headed', too, and consider if this may be relevant.

Camel

We identify camels with endurance: the ability to face hardship and survive due to inner resources. In material terms, camels are often also linked with financial gain. Emotionally, the symbolism is in the lack of feelings shown, perhaps the carrying of too much emotional baggage (maybe you need to forgive and forget), and to resourcefulness. One older interpretation links girls dreaming of camels to marriage (perhaps through the idea of partnership) and of the importance of keeping their husbands busy and not letting them get lazy! More spiritually, the camel enables us to travel through the desert, which suggests some sort of inner journey towards the emotional oasis you are seeking (see water entries, pages 178–83).

Cat

A lot depends here on how you feel about cats. They are quite a feminine animal, linked among cat lovers with caring or being cared for, and with intuitive understanding. If you are not a cat fan, their independence can be read as selfishness or even treachery, and an aggressive cat might be a sign of the dreamer not accepting their feminine side.

▶ **Black cats** have been linked with bad luck, magic (intuition) and also fear for centuries.

▶ **White cats** (especially kittens) have been linked to deceit, too.

Cow

Many dream interpreters in the past saw cows as a sign of prosperity and abundance – possibly of fertility. A more modern view would take into account their docile nature, suggesting passivity, and their role as mothers representing maternal instinct and being cared for.

▶ **Cow horns** are linked with the new moon, another symbol of femininity.

▶ **Cow milk** may link with images of maternity, or fertility (because it looks like semen).

Crab

Crabs can be tenacious, but are often seen in quite a negative way, suggesting you are clinging on to an idea that you should drop. Emotionally, we link crabs with irritability, suggesting difficulty in relationships – again, perhaps being too 'clingy' – and their shells suggest brittle, vulnerable feelings ('crabby'). The sideways movement of crabs suggests evasiveness.

Crocodile See Alligator.

Deer

Interpretations of deer are very positive. It is a symbol of fortune and friendship. The gracefulness and gentle nature of deer symbolize feminine qualities, although it is also seen as innocent to the point of being naïve.

▶ **A male deer** is seen as being independent and virile. Killing a deer indicates a wish to suppress these characteristics.

Dog

As man's best friend, a dog can, of course, represent the values of loyalty, companionship and devotion. This is just as well, as dogs are one of the most common animals seen in dreams. However, dogs can also be aggressive, and their barking can be seen as an indication of bad news to come. Dogs can also symbolize skills that have been neglected, and intuition (a dead dog, in particular, suggests that you are not using this skill).

▶ **A growling dog** may be a sign of your own inner conflict.

▶ **A dog on a lead** can be interpreted as some kind of restraint, especially of emotions (a black dog is a symbol of depression). In traditional tales, dogs often guard the gates of death or act as guides in the underworld.

▶ **Puppies** are identified with being carefree, perhaps to the extent of not being prepared for something.

Dolphin

The symbolism of dolphins has changed over the years. In 1830, one dream guide saw them as an omen of the death of someone close to you. Nowadays, we see dolphins in a much more positive light as a link with nature and a sign of trust (especially if you rode one), encouraging us to explore our spirituality and communicate in new ways. Because they swim effortlessly through water, dolphins suggest an ability to deal with emotional issues.

Donkey See Ass.

Elephant

Elephants are viewed very positively. They are powerful and dignified, suggesting stability. So, depending on the context, an elephant may represent success, or some sort of threat (from its power), and a need to be patient. Elephants famously never forget, so the animal could be a reminder of some long-lost memory. In some African cultures elephants represent wisdom and authority, and because they live a long time, we may well be identifying with an older generation.

Fish

Since fish inhabit water, the realm of the unconscious mind (see water entries, pages 178–83), they represent messages from our subconscious – insights brought up to the surface, which can, of course, be enlightening, soothing or threatening. So fish can represent a new understanding, and therefore dead fish suggest lack of insight or disappointment. The fish has also long represented Christianity and Christian beliefs, and eating fish has been linked with communion. It also has connections with sex and rebirth – sperm swim and are the catalyst for new life – while we all float in liquid in the womb before we are born.

Fox

Foxes are clever and untrustworthy. Dreaming of foxes suggests that there is someone in your life who you are wary of and who you feel may be insincere – a secret enemy. As a cunning predator, the fox hunts down what it needs. Were you the hunter or the prey: the ambitious seeker using its intuition and skills, or the hapless victim?

Frog

There is a huge range of interpretations of what frogs signify in dreams. This is a good example of how important it is to consider what frogs mean to you. Could it be a frog prince, something that is not quite what it seems, suggesting doubts about identity? Perhaps you think of the biological changes from frog spawn, to tadpole, to adult, which has obvious sexual connotations and could be linked to the idea of renewal.

Then again, frogs move by leaping, sometimes in unpredictable directions: is there a connection here with your life, such as a tendency to jump from one thing to another?

▶ **Toads** are seen in a darker, more sinister light.

Goat

Goats are survivors, showing sure feet on high rocky mountains. This could symbolize business or social success (those high places) through care and surefootedness. Goats also butt, so they represent enemies you want to keep an eye on. With its horns, hooves and hard eyes, the goat is often identified with the Devil, suggesting concerns about guilt and, possibly, sexual impulses. However, goats can also be sacrificial victims.

Horse

The horse is a symbol of power and sexuality. Horses are wild and strong: if you are controlling the horse, you are harnessing these characteristics, perhaps even taming them. Horses are frequently identified with wealth and prosperity, which is probably why one bank used a black horse in its advertisements. However, such horses also symbolize mystery and wildness. We also gamble on horses, so there may be an element of looking for a chance to do something. There is also a sexual connotation in riding a horse.

▶ **White horses** in particular have wild, romantic connotations – look for an emotional interpretation here.

▶ **Seeing a herd of wild horses** suggests a desire to be released from responsibilities and constraint.

Lamb

In the Bible, lambs are a symbol of innocence and purity. They are also often sacrificed to increase future wealth and good fortune. Being born in

must know

Children's animal dreams
Children frequently dream of animals, perhaps because they come across them as characters in books so often, and, of course, often have them as pets. Girls are more likely to dream about pets, and boys about wild animals. The key to interpreting the dream is to know how the child views the animal in question: some children are frightened of dogs, for example, so it will represent something they are afraid of.
▶ Is it a pet, in which case the dream may not be metaphorical?
▶ Have they met it in real life?
▶ Have they come across a similar animal in a book?

Monster

It is very common to dream of monsters at any age and they can provide valuable information about your inner thoughts. Monsters represent what you fear about yourself – your most negative, brutal or ugly tendencies. These could be a drink problem, a short temper, tearfulness, or anything else you (perhaps secretly) wish was different about you. If you are fighting the monster in your dream, this suggests conflict with the negative trait. If it is dominating you, you are struggling to deal with it and are feeling out of control.

spring, lambs also embody the idea of new life and being part of a life cycle. Remember also the phrase 'gentle as a lamb'.

Leopard

The leopard is a predator famous for its camouflage, so it represents a disguised threat or at least someone insincere. The leopard's spots can be interpreted as eyes, suggesting that you feel you are being watched. If the animal is caged, you feel in control of this situation.

Lion

Lions embody authority (after all, it is the king of the jungle), sexual dominance and fatherhood. So dreams about lions reflect how you cope with conflict, but the lion is also seen as proud and dignified, so there may be an element of admiration of the character it represents, or if it was you, a need for this. Dreaming of being chased by a lion in your house suggests you are trying to escape from your own powerful feelings.

Monkey

Monkeys mean mischief, which suggests you are concerned about the frivolous or deceitful side of your nature, or that of others in your life. The connotations are playful in a slightly evil way. In contrast, some believe that an engaged person who dreams of monkeys wants a speedy marriage.

Monster See common dreams box, above left.

Mouse

The mouse is famously timid, so represents fear and lack of assertiveness. Mice represent minor irritations that can build up if ignored. They tend to be identified with worries about domestic or business life. Mice also remind us of pubic hair, and as they slip in and out of holes there can be a sexual link too.

Oyster
Oysters have long been thought to be a very favourable dream omen, indicating a large and happy family, and great success in business and good health. Oysters are also identified with sexual gratification and indulgence, although their pearls can represent purity and humility. Because they have shells, oysters also suggest shutting out the world.

Pig
Pigs are not regarded very flatteringly in dreams, as they are seen as unclean and greedy. So they are identified with over-indulgence, selfishness and passion, which can suggest success in business (so it's not all bad news).

Rabbit
Rabbits are vulnerable, passive creatures, suggesting thoughts of the hurts one can suffer in life. They also, of course, breed like, well, rabbits, so there are undertones of fertility and joy. These animals have long been identified with good luck, so dreaming of them suggests an optimistic outlook.

Rat
Not exactly the most popular animal in the world, the rat represents enemies, possibly even your own business rivals. The fact that you are dreaming about them suggests doubt or guilt about something you are doing (not just at work – think of the phrase 'love rat'). Rats are identified with poverty, scavenging and being on the outside of society, so they reveal social and financial worries, of losing out in the 'rat race'.

Reptile
We tend to fear the cold, unblinking gaze of the reptile, and its unpredictable fast movements unsettle us, so the presence of a reptile, such as a lizard-type creature, indicates feelings that you are under threat, perhaps of betrayal. Reptiles also represent basic instincts. (See Alligator, Snake.)

did you know?

Snakes and molecules
German chemist Friedrich August Kekulé solved a major scientific problem through a dream. He was struggling to find the molecular structure of benzene and dreamed that he saw the molecules as a set of snakes. When one of them grabbed its own tail, Kekulé awoke with the realization that the structure was a ring.

Shark

Sharks are the world's greatest predator, and so they are a menacing figure in our dreams. Their cold, unblinking stare and ruthlessness also indicates worries about greedy, unscrupulous business colleagues – or your own feelings of hostility. As they inhabit water, the realm of the emotions, sharks can also represent painful or difficult emotions. The sharp teeth and powerful jaws of these fish also suggest fear of castration, of loss of power and influence.

Sheep

Old dream interpretations reflect the high value given to sheep in past times: they were a symbol of prosperity and advancement. Nowadays, we see sheep as lacking individuality and creativity, so in a dream they represent conformity and passivity.

Snake

From the Bible story of the Garden of Eden onwards, snakes have been the baddie in many a story. They encapsulate treachery and evil, and because they live on or below the surface, they represent your hidden fears. They are also phallic in shape and slide into holes, so can symbolize forbidden sexuality, or perhaps the fear that a partner is being unfaithful. As is often the way with dream interpretation, opposites can apply and snakes also have a healing role in some cultures (see the cult of Asclepius on page 30). For example, the Greek caduceus, a staff symbolizing medicine, was entwined with snakes, and some Indian yogis view the serpent as their spiritual guide.

Squirrel

Squirrels famously hoard food for hard times, so their presence in a dream suggests you either need to store more, or have too many reserves. Seeing squirrels running around suggests you feel an activity you are involved in is pointless or unprofitable.

Tiger

The tiger represents the more feminine side of the associations made with the lion. So the tiger can symbolize female sexuality and seduction. If it is attacking, you may be frightened of your own feelings. If it is caged, that is a sign of repressed emotions that may be about to surface.

Vampire

Vampires have a powerful symbolic resonance to do with fear, sex and feeling drained. We associate them with sensuality and death. The vampire may be a figure for someone in your life who is charming but sucking all the energy out of you, by being too demanding or controlling. Or you may be feeling physically or emotionally drained, as if the life is being sucked out of you. Vampire dreams can relate to sex and losing virginity but, equally, vampires are obsessive, so the dream may relate to some obsession to do with relationships or drugs. Vampires are powerful and evil, so the dreamer may be feeling overwhelmed by negative thoughts – there could be a moral dimension to these. Are you the exploited virgin?

▶ **If you are the vampire,** you are feeling that you are taking too much from others and behaving selfishly.

Wolf

Wolves signify hostility and violence. With its self-confident power the wolf also represents aggressive male sexuality. However, there is also a sense of mystery and pride, which suggests someone in control, even with social grace, and the wolf's undoubted strength of will is associated with ambition. The wolf can also be a symbol of solitude, suggesting concerns about companionship.

Birds

They fly where they choose and their lofty position offers an uninterrupted view of everything happening below them. From this it is clear that birds represent our imagination and intuition, and the ability to see clearly the situation we are in. They are also associated with feelings of joy, lack of inhibition, and liberation.

must know

Bird dreams

▶ Birds are even more positive images if they are brightly coloured and active – for example, singing and flying.

▶ Eggs are a symbol for money. Watch out for broken ones – they represent a loss!

▶ Birds flying high have long been seen as prophesying wealth.

▶ Killing a bird suggests loss of innocence.

Blackbird

For centuries, dreaming of blackbirds has been seen as a warning of deceit and trouble – unless they are flying or singing, when the meaning is reversed. As you will see in the section on colours in dreams (see pages 66–8), black is linked with the dark feelings of anxiety and unconscious urges.

Chicken

Chickens provide us with nourishment, and are, of course, a source of eggs, that symbol of new life. However, they are rather passive and chatter a lot, so tend to be associated with lack of willpower and excessive gossip.

▶ **A cock** symbolizes boastfulness and male sexual characteristics.

▶ **Cocks fighting** suggest family arguments.

▶ **A hen** is an image of passive blinkered motherhood.

Cormorant

These are traditionally signs of danger to sailors. They can also symbolize a false friend. Other interpreters see these birds as representing introspection and deep thinking.

Crane
Cranes are very positive, representing happiness, maternal love and inner harmony.

Crow
This is similar to the associations of the blackbird, but crows are very dark and very masculine, so they are linked with death and bad habits, particularly of men.

Cuckoo
'Cuckoo in the nest' describes an unwelcome visitor, and cuckoos represent feelings that your relationship is being invaded, or that you want to invade another relationship.

Dove
Since biblical times, doves have symbolized peace and tranquillity. White doves in particular represent innocence and loyalty. There is also a strong religious or spiritual element here – perhaps an encouragement to jettison negative thoughts.

Duck
Ducks have positive associations to do with journeys and domestic harmony, but you should consider also the phrase 'sitting duck'.
- ▶ **Flying ducks** are linked with spiritual growth.
- ▶ **Ducks on water** are usually suggestive of the unconscious mind.
- ▶ **Pairs of ducks** are a symbol of happy relationships.

Flamingo
Flamingos are usually seen in large groups, so in a dream they represent a sense of community and cooperation.

must know

Bird life stages
The life stages and situations of birds make ready associations with our own lives.
▶ **Hatching** suggests rebirth, and perhaps delayed plans.
▶ **A chick** represents our childhood.
▶ **The nest** suggests partnership and the home.
▶ **Leaving the nest** symbolizes independence and change.
▶ **Caged birds** show feelings of being trapped or restricted.
▶ **Dead birds** are associated with defeat and depression.

Goose

Geese fly together, suggesting lifelong relationships (especially motherly love) and conformity. The flying itself is linked with freedom and travel. Since we are familiar with seeing geese flying in formation on long journeys, there is a hint of anticipated change here, too. Geese are often linked to hopes of prosperity – did your goose lay a golden egg?

Hummingbird

This is a symbol of small ideas that may have great potential, or may be merely frivolous. Some see this as a sign of unwillingness to commit to relationships.

Ostrich

These birds famously bury their heads in the sand, suggesting someone is not facing up to the real world. It may also be a sign of feeling restricted and cut off.

Parrot

Parrots simply repeat what they hear, clearly denoting gossip, and possibly copying something without thinking it through. Because they are brightly coloured, a parrot also suggests someone who attracts attention in such a way that their talents do not merit.

Peacock

This bird's love of showing off its plumage suggests vanity and pride, or a desire for more colour and recognition in one's life. Peacocks are linked with prestige and success – but also with vanity and arrogance. It can be a symbol of new life as it sheds its feathers and grows them again.

Phoenix

This is obviously a symbolic creature, representing the ability to rise out of misfortune and succeed. It signifies our inner resources and ability to leave depression and death behind us.

Pigeon

Pigeons are known for their ability to return home, so can be a sign of success away from home. Pigeons also represent the arrival of news, bringing greater understanding.

Raven

They're black and rather sinister looking, with powerful beaks, so it's no surprise to learn that ravens are associated with feelings of disharmony, betrayal and danger.

Stork

The stork is traditionally associated with new life or the desire to be a parent.

Swan

These graceful and dignified birds have long been seen as good omens in dreams, especially of fertility. They also seem rather enigmatic, which has been linked to the idea that there is a mystery to be revealed, perhaps in our own unconscious. Remember also that 'swan song' means the final act, suggesting you feel something is about to end, especially a romance.

Vultures and buzzards

An unhappy image linked to death and isolation but also of not being able to come to terms with something – an ending of a relationship, perhaps, or a misunderstanding. Because these birds feed off others, you may be feeling you are being exploited, although a more positive spin on this is that you can 'feed' from your past experiences, gaining insights into a current problem.

Bodies

Because your body in a dream represents you, it can be an indication of how you see yourself: its size and condition reflects your self-esteem. Since what we dream comes from our own mind, it is suggested that dreams involving a certain body part can be literal, not symbolic. That body part may need attention.

must know

Bodies in dreams
When considering the meaning of a body part in a dream, think about its function and symbolic role – for example, we reach out to others with our arms, implying an emotional as well as a physical action.
▶ The left side of your body can be identified with confidence and feeling supported (reverse this if you are left-handed).
▶ Some analysts suggest the left side is the maternal influence on us, the right side the paternal one.

Anus

We release things we don't need through the anus, so dreams involving this part of the body are about getting rid of something, or failing to do so. Think first of all if you are pondering repressed or rejected feelings, remembering that the anus is a deeply personal part of your body (and so denotes your inner self). If excrement is involved, the dream is about something we consider unclean or hateful.

Arm

We reach out to others with our arms, so the dream could involve caring for people or needing comfort yourself. An injured arm suggests loss of confidence (perhaps the ability to ask for help or love) and a sense of helplessness. We make space for ourselves with our arms or even push people away with them, so the dream might indicate that you need some time to yourself, perhaps away from a relationship.
▶ **The right arm** represents your more aggressive, masculine side, and can also relate to strong moral issues.
▶ **The left arm**, in contrast, is more feminine and nurturing, perhaps linking with a need to grow and learn new skills.

Back

We 'put our back into' a big challenge requiring strength, possibly just strength of will. So dreams involving backs can be about facing new tasks and dealing with stress and pressure. The back determines our stance, how the world sees us, so the dream could concern attitudes to the dreamer or theirs to the outside world.

▶ **A bare back** symbolizes secrets.
▶ **A back turned to you** suggests rejection, possibly jealousy.
▶ **Carrying someone or something on your back** indicates feeling overwhelmed or used.

Beard

A beard was a symbol of wisdom and judgement to the ancient Egyptians. Nowadays a white beard has this meaning, but beards can also suggest something being concealed.

Blood

Blood is our liquid life force, so seeing someone lose blood is like watching the very essence of them disappear. Losing blood suggests the dreamer is being drained in some way, perhaps emotionally. Blood is also what we have in common with our relations, so there may be some issues to do with feelings or actions of the family.

Bones

Bones are hidden from sight, so they can represent personal secrets – perhaps skills not yet revealed openly. We talk about getting to the 'bare bones of something', indicating a wish to master the basics.

In dreams, bones also show our strength, so a broken bone reveals weakness. This could be a sign of a flaw in a plan, since bones are structures holding something up.

▶ **As a skeleton,** bones also suggest death.

Brain

The brain is the source of all our ideas, so it may represent a plan that has not received recognition. We solve problems with our brains, so dreaming about them suggests a feeling that there is something to be sorted out. As the symbol of reason, dreaming of it may be a call for a rational approach.

Breast

The breast symbolizes female sexuality and maternal love. Look at the context of the dream to decide whether it has a sexual element, or someone being nurtured.

Chest

Chests signify pride and confidence, and also emotion. If the chest is sunken, the dreamer may be feeling weakened in a conflict. A fuller chest is a sign of feeling prosperous and generous. Men tend to view the chest as a sign of social confidence. For women, it is more symbolic of womanhood.

Ear

Ears denote a need or desire to listen to others more carefully, to accept (perhaps unwelcome) advice.

▶ **Not hearing,** or having the ear blocked up, suggests a strong resistance to assistance.

▶ **Pain in the ear** suggests unwelcome news.

▶ **Someone with many ears:** believers in prophetic dreams hold that that person will have many happy employees, bringing great wealth.

Eye

We get most of our information through the eyes, so in dreams they represent knowledge and understanding. Thus a dream in which you have superb sight shows confidence in your actions, which diminishes according to any deterioration in vision. In life, we can also read a person's emotions through their eyes, so consider if they are hard and cold, or warm and open.

▶ **Having only one eye** suggests that you are not considering a situation in its entirety.

▶ **A third eye** is a sign of a need to look to yourself more.

▶ **Closed eyes** means refusal to face the facts, introversion.

▶ **Being blindfolded** indicates someone is hiding information from you.

▶ **Lack of eye contact** means lack of intimacy.

Face

The face represents both how we feel about ourselves, and how we want the world to see us, so seeing faces in a dream can supply a lot of information about your true state of mind.

▶ **Grotesque or ugly faces** show inner turmoil.

▶ **Cheeks** are symbols of intimacy, and rosy cheeks are a sign of vitality.

▶ **The forehead** is the sign of thought and judgement – so smooth is good, wrinkles suggest worries.

Foot

Feet give us stability and direction in life and can symbolize our most basic beliefs. In India, feet are the holiest part of the body, and are identified with divine qualities.

▶ **Bare feet** suggest feeling practical and 'grounded' – but in some cultures represent poverty.

▶ **Feet walking or running** indicates setting a new goal. For centuries, people have believed that dreams of washing your own feet are a bad omen of unrest.

Hair

Hair signifies self-image and attitudes. Dreams of having your hair cut are often noted as being anxious dreams.

▶ **Untidy hair** suggests confusion.

▶ **Brushing hair** shows you are trying to resolve this confusion.

▶ **Long hair** indicates feelings of liberation.

▶ **Very smart or tight hair** means discipline.

▶ **Dreaming of losing your hair** is often seen as an omen that something will be lost, perhaps of feeling un-empowered. In 1810, a seaman dreaming of having his head shaved would be told it was an omen of a shipwreck!

Hands and fingers

Hands show our relationships with others, especially at work, and so, not surprisingly, feature in many dreams. They are used for practical tasks, action and self-expression. As with arms, the left side represents feminine qualities, the right is more aggressive and masculine.

▶ **A clenched fist** shows anger and tension.

▶ **Tied hands** show difficulty in completing something.

▶ **Washing hands** shows worry or guilt – especially if washing away blood.

We work with our fingers, so in dreams fingers relate to how we feel we are doing our jobs.

▶ **Damaged fingers** symbolize an inability to achieve what we want, or to manipulate situations. Prophetic dream interpreters see hurt fingers as warnings of future conflict and losses.

Head

The head is the sign of intellect. How the head appears reflects the dreamer's state of mind:

▶ **Two heads** shows indecision.

▶ **A large head** shows confidence bordering on arrogance.

▶ **A small head** shows the opposite.

Heart

The heart is used as a symbol of feelings, courage and truth. The most common link is with the emotions, especially the need for love. Variations in the shape of the heart suggest insecurity in a romantic relationship.

Leg

Legs support and move the body, so in a dream they represent your own skills and ability to take control of situations.

▶ **Seeing someone else's legs** shows admiration for their confidence.

▶ **An injured or deformed leg** indicates a lack of balance in your life. Of course, we also move on our legs, so there may be some issue you are trying to run away from.

▶ **Knees** symbolize help from others. A bad knee suggests feelings of dissatisfaction with aid received from others, making you feel out of your depth.

▶ **Thighs** represent our ability to perform: if the thigh is not behaving normally, nor are you.

Mouth

Mouths are for communication, but we also use them to gain pleasure and nourishment:

▶ If you cannot open your mouth, there is something you feel unable to say, or regret saying.

▶ Chewing suggests thought.

▶ A closed mouth on another is a sign of death.

▶ The lips are the most sensual part of the mouth, so link with romance and sex – but can also indicate communication.

Neck

The neck links the head (thought, hopes) with the body (feelings and sexuality), and is also a vulnerable part of the body, showing weakness. So the neck represents the balance between your heart and head. Phrases such as 'up to your neck' and 'don't stick your neck out' indicate the neck as a limit to what you should do.

Teeth

Teeth are mentioned in a huge number of dreams because they are centre stage in a series of highly symbolic events and roles. Losing teeth and gaining new ones is part of childhood. The next time they fall out we are closer to death. They are vital tools for eating, carrying an aggressive bite, but also important to our attractiveness and self-esteem. Some dream interpreters believe teeth symbolize the words we utter – so rotten teeth mean lying. They can also symbolize the dreamer's overall appearance, their public face, and especially their ability to attract a partner. Teeth can show aggression, too – our ability to get want we want and keep it. Other meanings linked with teeth include:

▶ **Toothless people** are weak and ineffective – teeth have strong associations with power.
▶ **False teeth** mean just that: falsity.
▶ **A tooth that is being pulled out** implies birth.

▶ **An injured neck** suggests a clash between the heart and head. In the seventeenth century, you would have been told that a cricked neck was a sign that you felt ashamed of your actions.

Nose

Noses are a sign of intuition, as in the phrase 'follow your nose' for when we use our instincts, often to follow our own interests or curiosities. It can also be symbolic of the male sexual organ. Some people report that in dreams their nose grows as a punishment for lying, just like Pinnochio.

Penis

This is clearly to do with male sexuality, fertility and power. For men, dreaming about a penis can involve considering their life as a man and how they express their wants. A very large penis implies doubts about your own sexual performance. For women, the issue may be desire, but can widen to other male characteristics such as ambition.

▶ **Testicles** represent male sex drive and energy – having the 'balls' to get something done.

Skin

Our skin is what faces and touches the world around us. So skin in dreams represents sensitivity and protection.

▶ **Blemishes and rashes** suggest unwillingness to accept the real world, or of inadequacy.
▶ **Shedding skin** implies renewal.

Stomach

The stomach is hidden away, so dreams involving it may be dealing with repressed feelings. Since the stomach deals with digesting, or taking things in, dreaming about your stomach or abdomen suggests there is something you are having trouble accepting, such as change. Many dreams involving this part of the body involve being shot, perhaps because it is then exposed, emphasizing your vulnerability (and possibly trust).

Teeth See common dreams box, opposite.

Throat

We express ourselves through our throats, so it is linked to communication and imagination. A sore throat indicates difficulty in this.

Tongue

The tongue symbolizes speech. Dreaming of someone losing their tongue shows unresolved anger about something they said. The tongue also represents pleasure and new experiences.

Vagina

The vagina represents womanhood – including, but not exclusively, sexuality. It symbolizes the most fundamental feelings a woman has about relationships, sexual needs, the desire for children, and creativity. If the dream involves the uterus, it is about procreation issues.

did you know?

Bite-sized history
▶ **The Ancient Greeks** believed that the mouth symbolizes a house, and the teeth are those who live in it: men and the older inhabitants on the right, women and youth on the left. The oldest are the front teeth, while those in middle age have the eye teeth. Losing the tooth foretold the death of that person.
▶ **The Romans** believed the upper teeth represented householders, while the lower teeth were slaves.
▶ **By the seventeenth century** in the West, teeth were still identified with close family: upper teeth for males, lower teeth for females, front teeth for children and very close relations. Changes in size and condition suggested conflict with that part of the family.
▶ **Today,** some feel that a dream about teeth falling out implies fear of losing a close friend or relation.

Numbers, colours, shapes and symbols

We all have numbers that are significant to us (just ask anybody what numbers they would choose in a lottery) often linked to information such as house or telephone numbers. Likewise, colours and shapes carry a wealth of symbolism, like white weddings and Christian crosses.

must know

Numbers in dreams
▶ Numbers in dreams can just appear, but more often it is a question of counting how many people or significant objects there are, or how many times the same events happen in the dream.
▶ So consider first if the number has a special meaning for you: could it be an anniversary, pin number or address?
▶ Symbolic numbers are usually less than ten, but if a larger one is apparent, try adding the digits until you get a single digit number. For example, 152 is 1 + 5 + 2 = 8.
▶ Odd numbers are thought of as more aggressive and masculine than calm, balanced, feminine even numbers. The numbers described in this section are those that crop up most and that are considered to have a general significance.

Numbers

▶ **Zero:** Zero is a void – and with nothing there, you have the freedom to do what you like with no restrictions. Some interpreters believe that as it is round, it is a female shape, others that because it represents the universal void, it is God. Zero on the end of other numbers increases their power tenfold. (See also Circle.)

▶ **One:** Being on its own, one is individual – which could be a leader, or someone very isolated, or both. One can represent selfishness and/or creativity, and there is a possible phallic symbolism.

▶ **Two:** The number two can indicate balance and sharing, or disagreement and obstacles – we see it as a coming together, or that we are 'in two minds'. It may represent a doubling of something else in the dream, which could be a weakness or a strength.

▶ **Three:** Three has many positive connotations: parents with a child; the past, present and future; the trio of Father, Son and Holy Spirit; mind, body and spirit. So it tends to be identified with creativity and energy. Some interpreters see three as our inner self, or intuition, communicating. To Freud, it represented the male genitals.

▶ **Four:** This number represents stability and security, suggesting completion. It is seen as a sign for success, especially in business. There are also four seasons, points of the compass and the elements (water, air, fire and earth).

▶ **Five:** Five is commonly linked to our five senses, through which we experience everything. It is an encouragement to follow your hopes and beliefs.

▶ **Six:** Six is often identified with family love. It suggests harmony and balance.

▶ **Seven:** Seven is the number for spirituality and the sense of completion – for example, it is the number of days in the week, colours in the rainbow, different notes in a scale, the ancient heavenly bodies. It is significant as a measurement of life, as we use a seven-year cycle and celebrate adulthood at 21.

▶ **Eight:** Eight is often identified with material success, such as completing deals and increasing authority.

▶ **Nine:** Nine can be linked to childbirth as it is the duration of pregnancy in months, and some feel it therefore denotes great productivity, or humanity as a whole.

▶ **Ten:** Ten suggests completion, the ending of something and a new beginning. It may also be linked to the Ten Commandments, the first laws.

▶ **Eleven:** The eleventh hour is close to a deadline, and eleven is between the number of commandments and of disciples, giving it unhappy connotations of being beyond the law and incomplete.

▶ **Twelve:** There were 12 disciples and there are the same number on a jury, so there is an idea of spiritual support and judgement in this number.

▶ **Thirteen:** In the West, 13 has long been considered unlucky. This is not so in other cultures: Mexicans, for example, see it as lucky because their ancestors centuries ago believed there were 13 gods and the same number of heavenly bodies. It is often seen as a number for transitions (the 13th month is the start of the new cycle, for example).

▶ **Twenty-one:** This number represents the coming of adulthood with all its responsibilities.

Colour in dreams
► When interpreting colour, consider first its meaning for you. Is it the colour of a favourite childhood toy, or of the door of an enemy?
► Think carefully about where the colour appears – is it refining the symbolism of an animal, place or person, for example?
► Another factor is how the colour is made up: orange is a blend of fiery, passionate red and happy, positive yellow.
► Coloured skies suggest that this is something the dream is aspiring for, as it is above them.
► Consider also whether colours are together: red and grey together suggest deep depression, for example, with the depth coming from the red and the sadness from the grey.

Colours

► **Beige:** Beige is a neutral colour, suggesting detachment – which may indicate isolation, or, more positively, a sense of perspective.

► **Black:** A very common colour in dreams, black is dark and mysterious, carrying associations with death, depression and hate – suggesting conflict. In dreams it is often associated with the unconscious mind, and, with its disregard for life, recklessness. At the very least, it brings a sense of sadness and despair to a dream. Dreaming in black and white suggests two extreme viewpoints, and a need to find a compromise between them.

► **Blue:** Blue is another common dream colour, and can sometimes be linked with the high aspirations of the sky, or the deep emotions of the sea. However, the shade of blue can be significant. Light blue tends to be associated with spirituality and intuition: it is a contented and optimistic, if cool colour. Dark blues are more threatening, especially to women, as they suggest an unpredictable or changeable character. If a person is wearing dark blue clothing, this shows your lack of trust in them.

► **Brown:** As with blue, the shade of brown is significant. Brown is a serious, 'down to earth' (literally) colour, putting things in their most basic, bare form. Dark brown indicates dullness and lethargy, suggesting indecisiveness and decay. Light brown is more positive as it is associated with rejuvenation and freedom.

► **Burgundy:** This is a rich colour suggesting prosperity, courage and power.

► **Gold:** This signifies something you value highly,

not necessarily in a materialist way, but possibly spiritually.

▶ **Green:** Green is the colour of health and healing, with associations of growth, vitality and peace. It is an indication of feeling positive about change – which can, of course, also suggest naivety. Green can also symbolize independence. The darker the green, the less positive its meaning, as dark green is the colour of envy and suspicion – and, remember, jealousy is green.

▶ **Grey:** This is an unhappy, dull colour, suggestive of fear and being distanced from feelings.

▶ **Indigo:** This colour is linked with spiritual feelings and intuition.

▶ **Orange:** Orange is a passionate colour with strong spiritual associations. It suggests an interest in new activities, people and ideas. As an attractive blend of warm red and happy yellow, it symbolizes harmony and balance, the ability to assimilate. Some interpreters associate it with reproductive health and sexuality.

▶ **Pink:** Pink is a healthy, optimistic colour, full of tenderness and femininity. Strong, hot pinks carry stronger sexual connotations.

▶ **Purple:** Purple is the colour of royalty, suggesting nobility and dignity. In dreams, it can represent higher social rank, something the dreamer may aspire to, or dislike. For some, it has spiritual associations, especially in the Catholic Church.

▶ **Red:** Red is a vibrant, warm colour, suggesting energy, passion and sometimes aggression. It is also the colour of blood and shame, and is used in nature and on 'stop' signs as a warning. Red is earthy and basic, symbolic of sexual desire (especially red clothes), and fertility. So, try to decide if it was the evil red of the Devil or the energetic hue of fire and blood.

▶ **Turquoise:** This is a healing colour often associated with completing something successfully, so it has traditionally been seen as a good omen.

▶ **Violet:** See Indigo.

▶ **White:** White is the colour dreamers mention most often in their dreams, perhaps because sometimes it indicates an absence of colour (suggesting sadness, desolation or a ghost). It represents purity, dignity and clarity of thought – perhaps a new outlook. White clothes are obviously linked with marriage. Eastern cultures associate white with death and mourning. For dreaming in black and white, see Black.

▶ **Yellow:** As always, context is everything in dream interpretation. In happy dreams, a sun-like yellow symbolizes energy, hopefulness and confidence. If the dream is unhappy, the association is with caution (or indecisiveness) and even sickness if the yellow is pale.

Shapes and symbols

▶ **Ball:** A ball is a three-dimensional circle, and shares that shape's associations with perfection, suggesting a rounded, fully developed character. However, it also has sexual connotations with testicles and breasts. There may also be an echo of childhood playing with a ball.

▶ **Circle:** The circle has no beginning or end: it is the eternal cycle of life. Some interpreters see it as representing ourselves as a whole. Freudians argue it is a vagina. The circle protects and imprisons – so consider the whole context of your dream.

▶ **Crescent:** A crescent represents the skills of female creativity and versatility.

▶ **Cross:** See page 128.

▶ **Cube:** A cube can be a house, which in dream imagery represents the self. It is also symbolic of wisdom and perfection. As a die with numbers on each side, it highlights the many uncertainties of life.

▶ **Diamond:** A diamond shape points in four directions, showing that choices can be made.

▶ **Line:** We 'draw a line' under something when we no longer wish to discuss it. However, lines also show movement in both space or time, and so can mark a boundary.

▶ **Mandala:** A mandala is a square or circle enclosing other shapes or symbols. It is a positive sign symbolizing unity, spirituality and harmony. It suggests the dreamer has found balance between the diffuse parts of their character in their life.

▶ **Pyramid:** To the ancient Egyptians, the pyramid provided the link between earth and the heavens, and to the creative power of the sun. So it can symbolize wider awareness and its integration into the self. To Freudians, it is also a phallus.

▶ **Sphere:** See Ball.

▶ **Spiral:** This has a number of possible meanings. Events in our lives can 'spiral out of control', but the spiral is also a series of circles suggesting repetition and movement towards some goal, like a new idea. Some believe that a spiral rotating clockwise takes us to higher ideals, while the opposite direction is towards the unconscious.

▶ **Square:** A square is stable (perhaps to the point of stagnation) and balanced. It could represent the four walls of a house, and therefore the self.

▶ **Star:** See page 145.

▶ **Triangle:** The triangle unites three ideas. Take your pick from body, mind and spirit; father, mother and child; the Father, Son and Holy Spirit; body, experience and consciousness. Freud saw it as a symbol of the sexual organs (pionting up for males, down for females).

must know

Shapes and symbols in dreams

▶ Shapes and symbols are efficient ways of communicating ideas and information – look at how road signs allow us to 'read the road', or consider the phrase 'a picture is worth a thousand words'. So, any shape or symbol in your dream is carrying a powerful message from your subconscious.

▶ Objects in the centre of a shape are being given especial importance. Their opposites or rivals will be at the edges.

▶ Try to remember if the shape or symbol remained intact, broke up or changed in some other way. Consider this in your interpretation.

Events and activities

This section deals with things happening in your dream, whether they are actions you are involved in or events that are part of the whole scenario. Consider if they have echoes with your life so far, or if their meaning is likely to be entirely symbolic.

Accident

People are often understandably concerned if they have an accident in a dream, fearing it is a premonition, but there is no evidence that this is the case. Accidents are signs of anxiety, sometimes guilt that you deserve to be punished for something. The location of the accident will be symbolic. For example, road accidents may be a warning that you are 'driving yourself too hard', and household accidents will relate to your personality.

Affair

The dream could relate to feelings of betrayal or distrust within your relationship. However, dreams about cheating on a partner or spouse are quite common, and may be a useful release for thoughts that might otherwise lead to actions that you would regret. Assuming that the dream is not one of 'wish fulfilment' (which, of course, it could be), the affair may be about you connecting with other aspects of yourself, so consider what the other person was like and what characteristics they could represent. It is quite possible that the dream is showing you a fantasy of how you would like to behave with your partner, and is actually affirming the relationship.

Biting

Biting others is a sign of aggression; you are repressing your anger towards someone. Being bitten indicates vulnerability (see box – Teeth – on page 62).

Captivity

Who captured you and what was your relationship like with your captor? If you cooperated, he or she represents someone who dominates you in real life. Some analysts argue that being held in a small room is a return to the womb, suggesting maternal dominance. Others suggest that being held captive prevents you moving on, so your captor fears your development. Being a victim takes away your own responsibilities so you may be frightened of some new challenge. Being captive might also suggest feeling trapped in a situation in your everyday life. (See also Escape, Kidnapping.)

Chase See common dreams box, right.

Choking

Choking suggests that you feel unable to express yourself clearly. It also indicates indecision. If you are choking others, see Violence.

Crying

Crying when dreaming is likely an emotional release. If you cry in the dream and no one responds, you are feeling unsupported and frustrated.

Dancing

Dancing suggests freedom, harmony and sexual desire. Consider the style of dancing – if it seemed

---

common dreams

Chase

Being chased is a common anxiety dream. Your pursuers represent either other people who you feel persecuted by, or elements of your own personality that you are trying to repress – in which case the dream will repeat until you resolve the issue. Try to establish the emotional content of the dream.

▶ **Being chased by animals** indicates either anxiety about that animal, perhaps from some childhood incident, or by what they represent to you (see the animals section on pages 42–51 for more guidance). The main issue will be emotional.

▶ **Being chased by strangers** reveals your paranoia.

▶ **Being chased by the opposite sex** indicates fear of love or sex.

▶ **Chasing another person** suggests you are worried that someone you know is making a mistake, and you want to correct them.

good to know

Myoclonic jerk
A lot of people report experiences in which they commence a falling dream just as they are nodding off, then wake up with a jolt. This is known as a myoclonic jerk or spasm. What happens is that your brain sends out a message to the muscles, which have relaxed in anticipation of sleep, and you suddenly return to full consciousness. However, if you were dreaming of falling, you naturally assume you were awakened by the fear you experienced. In fact, you should be able to drop off to sleep almost immediately.

more ceremonial and you were alone, there may be associations with ancient rituals, which would indicate you are seeking spiritual release. Did you feel comfortable with the dance? If not, there may be an imbalance between your desire for intimacy and your feelings. Other people dancing suggests you desire them.

Digging

If you are digging, you are trying to find something. What you find will be highly symbolic, probably linked to feelings or memories. It also indicates hard work and if you were alone, your subconscious may be telling you to slow down.

Disappearance

In the magical dream world, anything can vanish at any time as your subconscious manipulates your thoughts. People disappearing suggests insecurity about your relationship with them, and that you cannot rely on them. Whatever objects disappear or reappear will be symbolic.

Disaster

People often dream of natural disasters such as floods and earthquakes, and these memorable episodes are triggered by how we feel about changes in our waking life. Disasters also reveal a fear of losing control. Much will depend on how you coped with the disaster in your dream, and your role in your survival – did someone help you or were you the rescuer?

▶ **Earthquakes:** a dream where the ground is not stable shows emotional insecurity. You are uncertain of your 'ground'. Some interpreters see earthquakes as being about the physical aspects of your life – money, work.

▶ **Floods:** See page 179.

▶ **Tidal waves:** suggest massive emotional upheaval, and sexual feelings you cannot control.

▶ **Tornados:** linked with rage and loss of temper, again linked to the emotions.

Diving

Diving suggests overcoming anxiety and being prepared to take a risk. By diving in, you are showing commitment to dealing with an issue. What was the water like? Refer to Water section (pages 178–83) for more help.

Escape

This may show that you feel freed from limitations, but a more negative slant is that you are running away from your responsibilities – consider the whole dream to decide. How you managed to escape will be very meaningful – you may have discovered a new skill, or stopped doing something that was holding you back. (See also Captivity.)

Exam See common dreams box: Test, page 78.

Explosion

Any wild blast of energy suggests a loss of temper, anger and displeasure. Because the ground moves, there may be social upheaval. It may also symbolize an orgasm.

Falling See common dreams box, above.

common dreams

Falling
Very many people have dreamed that they are falling, often waking up feeling terrified. There are a number of interpretations, but the majority link falling with anxiety about not coping and being helpless, and feeling out of control and perhaps inferior. This lack of security could, of course, be linked with many aspects of your life – emotional, financial, work, etc. Other interpretations of falling include: sexual indulgence – as in 'fallen women'; a childhood memory of falling from bed; feelings of loss of status; loss of control, leaving you in a difficult situation from which you are trying to escape. This implies a (figurative) need to stay on solid ground and be very practical.

Fighting See Violence.

Fire

There are a number of meanings available for this common dream. Some believe that fire dreams can be induced by the dreamer being over hot (an organic dream). However, as fire destroys and purifies, the circumstances of the dream are crucial. Fire is also identified with passion, sexuality and anger – 'hot' states. It can represent your drives and motivation.

▶ **Passing through fire** indicates the dreamer is purified and renewed.

▶ **Being burned** suggests you are suffering because of your hot temper.

▶ **Whatever is burning** will be symbolic. For example, a house fire will relate to feelings about the home (see Homes and houses on page 118).

Hiding

This means you are avoiding something, perhaps out of guilt. You may be protecting something or some feeling that could be under threat. It could be an attempt to avoid responsibility. What are you hiding from in the dream?

Hunting

Hunting is a basic animal instinct. You are following an inner desire, and since hunting has associations with conquest, it could be sexual. Whatever you are hunting will have symbolic value – it could represent part of yourself. Being hunted indicates fear of failing.

Intercourse See Sex.

Kidnapping

This indicates loss of security and control. It is a powerful image because the dreamer is a helpless victim – and this may be attractive to some because it deprives you of responsibility. (See also Captivity.)

Kiss

Kissing shows acceptance, in addition to the obvious connotations of affection and sex.

► **A dream ending just before a kiss** indicates uncertainty about the relationship.

► **Kissing someone of the same sex** may be a homosexual fantasy but could also be showing acceptance of your masculine/feminine side.

► **Watching other people kiss** is intrusive and suggests you are too involved in the relationships of others.

► **Kissing an opponent** suggests duplicity.

Lightning

Lightning is a flash of brilliance – maybe a startling insight through increased consciousness. It can also represent energy and shock, probably linked to unexpected change. The force of lightning suggests the release of some pent-up feeling, which may be destructive. There may also be a sexual element to this dream (lightning represents sperm) and there may be a connection with death (see Death on page 129).

Losing something

Leaving aside the possiblility that you really have lost something, this is about losing something of symbolic value: it could be a relationship, integrity or something to do with your own identity. If this dream occurs regularly and involves losing personal things, it could represent your uncertainty about how you conduct your life, or worry about being disorganized.

Masturbation

If you do not fulfill your sexual (and indeed, other) needs, they will emerge through your subconscious, so dreaming of masturbation (or finding that you are) is simply your body finding a way to get what it wants. How you feel about that depends on your attitude to sexuality and pleasuring oneself.

Nudity See common dreams box, page 76.

Packing

This is a dream about moving on. You could be preparing to deal with a big change in your life. Alternatively, the packing could be of your

common dreams

Nudity

Going about your everyday life and suddenly finding you are naked is an extremely common dream. When we are naked, we show vulnerability. You may be showing a wish to be seen for what you are, revealing your true nature. This is more likely if you are usually a very guarded, private person. However, given that we tend to hide our bodies even from those we are familiar with, it is possible that the dream is about having your weaknesses exposed and exploited. After all, Adam and Eve became ashamed by their nakedness. There could be something you are worried about being found out about or maybe it is an anxiety dream about not being prepared. Perhaps you are trying to be something that does not meet your true identity? Alternatively, the dream could be a fantasy about getting attention or rebelling against society.

'emotional baggage', which you need to put behind you. You may feel your life is too hectic and you need to put some activities on hold. This is especially likely if you repeatedly dream of packing and unpacking, although another interpretation here is that you are being indecisive. The most positive take on this dream is that you are asserting your independence.

Painting

Creative activities are about self-expression and in dreams this can include ideas springing up from the subconscious that we were not aware of. Look carefully at the content of the painting. If you are decorating, you may be trying to brighten up your life (see Homes on pages 118–19) or how others see you. You could also be trying to cover something up. (See also Colours, pages 66–8.)

Paralysis See page 83.

Rape

This is an upsetting dream about being overpowered and violated, but it may not necessarily be about sex. The issue could be about being powerless in your own life to the extent that you hardly feel human.

▶ **If the attacker is faceless**, the dream could reveal that you feel totally exploited.

▶ **Being the attacker** in such a dream indicates unresolved anger.

▶ **Watching a rape** indicates a sense of powerlessness and of being a victim in some way.

Running

Decide whether you were running towards something (positive) or away from something (negative). On the plus side, running is a sign of vitality and good motivation. The negatives are:

▶ **Running away** shows fear. You are trying to avoid an issue.
▶ **Running aimlessly** indicates lack of direction and a need to slow down.
▶ **Being unable to run** shows low confidence.

Sex

Many dreams involve sex, and many of these are simply a result of the human desire to have sex – wish fulfilment or memory. The dream may just reveal a wish to enjoy a more adventurous sex life. Sex with someone other than your current mate indicates concern over that relationship. This is especially common among couples approaching marriage, and is a natural sign of anxiety over the major step they are taking. However, sex dreams can have other meanings too. Consider the nature of the dream, who seemed to be in control, whether the actions were taboo, and how you were feeling: it may be about power and being in control; it may be about how we think people see us. Dreaming about sex can also mean a need for creative expression.

▶ **Watching others have sex** can reveal your own concern about sexual interaction. This dream is more common among women than men, who are generally participating in the dream.
▶ **Homosexual sex** dreams could be about you finding and being comfortable with your masculine or feminine side.
▶ **Dreaming about weird or taboo sex** doesn't mean you are a pervert: you are exploring your sexuality without risk and without hurting anyone. In dreams we drop the complicated social rules of our waking lives, so relax!
  (See also Affair.)

Sleeping

Dreaming that someone is asleep suggests that some part of the dreamer is unconscious or repressed. If the dreamer is the sleeper, they are isolating themselves from something or someone.

common dreams

Test

Taking a test or exam and realizing you are not prepared for it (or that it is impossible, for example the paper is in a foreign language or the questions are invisible) is a very common dream. It may, of course, relate to a forthcoming exam, but more frequently is an anxiety dream about not meeting people's expectations of you. You are hoping to gain acceptance and are afraid of rejection for not being good enough. Your subconscious fears you may be unprepared for your next challenge. It is asking you to look to yourself and pay more attention to some latent skill or feeling that needs cultivating. You may also be devoting too much energy to pleasing others.

Speech making

It is very common to dream of having to make a speech in public. This dream has similar meanings to that of realizing you are naked: fear of inadequacy.

Sports

Sports represent challenges and a test of our virility. We identify playing sport with setting and achieving goals, teamwork and competitiveness. There is also a sexual element in the way games build up to climactic moments, and most games carry a Freudian's delight of sexual symbols.

▶ **Individual sports** such as golf have associations with independence.

▶ **Team games** reveal a desire for there to be more social interaction in your life.

▶ **Risky sports** such as skiing suggest a craving for adventure.

▶ **The referee** is often a father figure.

Stealing

Stealing in a dream suggests that you feel guilty about some action in your waking life. This has associations with feeling unloved or undeserving (thus no one will give you anything and you'll have to steal). You are also showing jealousy of others. Being a victim of theft indicates feelings of injustice and fear of loss.

Test See common dreams box, above.

Touching

Touching someone shows a need for intimacy and communication. This is a relationship you want to develop, possibly sexually.

▶ **If there is no touching** in a scenario where you would expect it, you are revealing a lack of ability to express yourself and reach others.

▶ **Actively avoiding contact** means you were showing animosity to this person.

Violence

Many dreams are unpleasant, and few more so than the extremely graphic violence many people witness in their sleep. There is clearly an extreme emotion that has been repressed and is released in the dream state. Consider carefully who the violence was directed at and by whom, and the other circumstances. The dream may be a reference to a past fight, perhaps in childhood. Common feelings associated with violence are domination and control, anger and feeling victimized. In about half of dreams where the dreamer is beaten, they do not recognize their attacker, who is therefore likely to be an archetype (see the box on Jungian archetypes on page 28). They will represent certain relationships or fears.

▶ **Violence directed at an authority figure:** the dream is providing an outlet for your frustration.

▶ **Fights** usually show some inner conflict within your psyche.

▶ **Watching others fight** indicates being involved in a conflict that you are not trying to resolve.

▶ **An attack by an animal** suggests fear of one's own instincts.

(See also Weapon on page 147.)

must know

Indian omens
According to the Indian *Sacred Books of Wisdom*, or *Veda*, dating from before 1000 BC, if the dreamer is active in trying to deal with violence in a dream, he will find success and happiness in the future. If the dreamer is passive and gets hurt, the meaning is reversed.

Walking

Walking slows the action, and suggests a desire to take some time out from daily tribulations. If you are moving with ease, you feel content with your progress through life. Difficulties suggest obstacles or hesitation.

Weather

Weather helps to set the mood for a dream, which is always important. The weather usually reveals your feelings about the world around you, and whether it is in harmony with you. (See also Disaster and Rain on page 180 and Snow on page 181.)

Feelings

Feelings encountered in a dream can be alarmingly intense, leaving the dreamer bewildered by an emotional experience and wondering what triggered it. These feelings are very likely to be a reflection of your waking life, including emotions that you were hardly aware of – your inner fears or repressed anger.

must know

Feelings in dreams
Consider the overall context of the dream.
▶ What was your general mood?
▶ Were strong feelings triggered by particular events or people, and if these are not part of your everyday life, what could their symbolic meaning be?
▶ Releasing repressed emotions is generally thought to be healthy, so the fact that you felt great anger in a dream could be helping you to resolve some issue.
▶ If you can never remember feelings in a dream, you may be cutting your emotional self off from the world, to avoid hurt.

Abandoned

This feeling doesn't necessarily mean the dreamer is feeling isolated. It could indicate a feeling of dependence on someone, or vice versa, and the reverse is dreamt of. You may also be abandoning an aspect that you no longer need or want. Feeling lost suggests a lack of purpose in your own life, and perhaps difficulty in making choices – you are finding it hard to navigate the journey of your own life.

Aggression

This suggests conflict. You may feel you have been too passive and need to 'have your say'. The tension may be sexual – something is being repressed here.

Alone

Feeling alone suggests isolation, but, of course, we can be alone by choice, so you may be taking some time out to gather new energy. There are also periods in our lives when we feel more alone, for example in adolescence, and this may refer back to that.

Anger

Consider what or who the anger is directed at. Being

angry in a dream suggests that you are not releasing this feeling in your waking life. This could be very healthy – you may be releasing tension by imagining 'letting go' rather than actually doing something that can be very destructive. Alternatively, you could simply be feeling frustrated and trapped. Think carefully about what led to this feeling in the dream.

Anxiety

Many people remember feeling anxious in their dream. This may be because strong emotions are more memorable than less extreme ones. The anxiety could relate to difficulties in your everyday life, or something you feel is lurking below the surface: find out what triggered the feeling and look into its symbolism.

Blindness

This suggests that you either cannot, or will not, be aware of something in your own life (which includes your inner life). The dreamer is feeling vulnerable, unclear of their direction, and possibly fearful of being misdirected by others. Freud linked blindness to a male fear of castration – which can, in turn, be linked with doubts about your sexuality.

Confusion

Apart from bewilderment at a choice you have in life, confusion can also indicate that your mind is seeking some memory from your past that will help you now. Try to identify what triggered the confusion.

Crying

Crying releases negative emotions, which you may be holding back in your waking life – so crying in a dream can be very therapeutic. Try to identify what caused the weeping. Crying can indicate guilt at something you yourself have done.

Fear

Fear is a common feeling experienced in dreams. Consider exactly what triggered this feeling in your dream, and its symbolic role. Fear of darkness suggests a concern that you are not fully informed about something in your waking life. Fear can also indicate self-doubt or lack of trust in others.

Guilt

A sense of guilt suggests that you feel you do not deserve to have achieved what you have so far, so it is linked to self-esteem. You may be feeling guilty about some repressed desire.

Happiness

A sense of happiness in a dream suggests just that: a dream. Your subconscious is trying to compensate for feelings of stress and sadness. Disconcertingly, people who have suffered bereavement can have dreams of great happiness – but the message is a contrary one.

Jealousy

Envy in a dream indicates your own insecurities about a person or feeling. It also indicates that you are closed off from someone, fearful of intimacy and not able to show your vulnerability.

Laughter

Laughing in a dream suggests a need to be more spontaneous and to follow your intuition more. You may also be feeling guilty about something. If the laughter is directed at you, you are feeling 'got at'.

Love

Unless your feelings of love in a dream match those of your waking life, you are dreaming of love as compensation for not getting it. Consider what kind of love you felt in the dream:

▶ **Young love,** where you are besotted and dependent, or it is unrequited.

▶ **Adolescent love,** which is full of uncertainties.

▶ **Adult love,** where you accept you and your partner's needs.

Other meanings for dreams about love may relate to your feelings about sex, marriage and self-expression. Lustful dreams, for example, indicate you are feeling unfulfilled.

Pain

Pain in a dream (which can feel amazingly real) may relate to a genuine problem in your body (see pages 56–63). Causing pain to yourself in a dream suggests you are trying to avoid reality by putting up obstacles. Consider the type of pain: is it from within or outside, is it a wound, infection or even an amputation?

Panic

This shows a feeling that things are out of control and disempowered. Try to establish the cause and what, if anything, was stopping you from dealing with it.

Paralysis See common dreams box, above.

Rejection

Dreaming of rejection suggests you cannot accept some situation in your waking life. Doing the rejecting yourself implies there is something you want to eject from your own life.

Sick

Dreaming that you are sick in some way shows internal conflict in your life, about which you are feeling victimized.

Suffocation

This frightening dream is often related to feelings of lack of self-expression. You may feel smothered in a relationship or you may be feeling stressed.

Vulnerable

Dreaming that you are vulnerable and need to be saved indicates your wish for someone else to make things right. Your vulnerability may take the form of being unable to talk, being handicapped or tied up, or being almost naked. Look at the rest of the dream to discern the source of your concern. Who helped you or did you manage on your own?

common dreams

Paralysis
This is caused by fear in your real life, most probably of change – so lack of confidence could be an element. There may be some internal conflict that is causing you to 'seize up' in some way. Your subconscious may have created a situation to which you have reacted in an unexpected way, and your rational side has stopped the action to try to make sense of it.

Food

It is very common to dream about food. The first thing to consider is how you regard that food. Is it a childhood favourite or something you have always despised? Sometimes, of course, dreaming about a food is caused by hunger, but food also suggests thoughts and beliefs that you need to mentally digest.

must know

Food in dreams
▶ The shape and colour of foods can be highly symbolic, especially those that resemble the genitals (see Fruit).
▶ If food tastes bad in a dream, this indicates that the dreamer is unhappy at him or herself.
▶ Buying or gathering food indicates ambition, planning and work.
▶ Cooking food is a sign of prosperity and generosity.
▶ Eating food relates to the dreamer's health, and to relationships with others.
▶ Large quantities of foods such as peas, grain and corn suggest wealth and abundance.

Apple
In the Bible, an apple represents knowledge, and (through sexual knowledge) sin – it is, after all, the forbidden fruit. However, apples are now mostly seen in a positive light as a sign of love, fertility and prosperity, or possibly as indicating a desire to return to more innocent, less troubling times.
▶ **Green apples** represent love that has yet to flourish, or other ventures that may not eventually come to fruition.
▶ **Rotten or half-eaten apples** represent carelessness or ill feeling.
▶ **Stealing apples** suggests a wish for an illicit sexual relationship.

Apricot
Different interpreters see apricots as either omens of misfortune, or a sign of marriage. Some readers may see no difference between these messages!

Banana
These have a clear phallic symbolism, but they can also represent isolation or fragility.

Biscuit

These are a pleasure from childhood, so the dream is taking you back to this time.

Bread

Dreamers frequently report that they dreamt of bread, often with water. As a staple food, bread represents the basic needs of life and the learning we all achieve through experience. As a basic need, bread can also symbolize sex. We 'break bread' together, so bread can represent companionship and fellowship.

▶ **Stale bread** signifies an opportunity the dreamer did not exploit fully.

▶ **Toasted bread** is often a comfort food and shows a need to be cosseted at home.

▶ **Burnt toast** can symbolize a broken home.

▶ **Bread with water or wine** carries a spiritual message, with water representing purification, and wine the blood of Christ.

Butter

This symbolizes the ending of a fast and so is seen as an optimistic omen. The eating of butter in a dream has long been seen as a sign of a forthcoming legacy.

Cake

Cake is comfort food but it is also usually shared, so in a dream it can represent a need or desire to share something – to lessen your load, or to gain benefits that others are receiving.

▶ **Eating cake** can denote sensual enjoyment.

▶ **Baking cakes** signifies productivity.

must know

Drinking
Liquids symbolize the life force, so when drinking we are 'taking in' or trying to understand that force – here, then, is a dream about the fundamentals of life. The act of drinking may also show a desire to be part of a social scene.

▶ **A wedding cake** symbolizes the future, with all its joys and responsibilities – are you looking up at it as if it is a mountain to climb, or down from it, as if you have already achieved much?

Carrot

A carrot could be a symbolic reward (instead of the 'stick'), and also signifies hard work. Like other vegetables, it can also denote abundance.

Cheese

Dreaming of cheese has signified profit and gain since at least 1695.

Chocolate

We tend to reward ourselves with chocolate, so to dream of it is to congratulate yourself on your achievements – with just a hint that you may be overindulging in something.

Corn

Corn is a traditional symbol representing both abundance and growth.

Cornflakes

Television commercials create an image of idyllic family life around cornflakes and other breakfast cereals, which may have a subconscious influence our dreams.

Dessert

Like other comfort foods, this represents a need for support from others. Large, extravagant desserts also suggest enjoyment of the good things in life, and either reward or temptation, depending on the dreamer's attitude to the food.

Egg

These are symbols of birth and creation. For men, they can represent motherhood, possibly even the dreamer's mother.

▶ **Eggs breaking** symbolize need for care in this relationship, and vulnerability in other areas of life.
▶ **Brightly coloured eggs** represent happy events.
▶ **Rotten eggs** signify loss, or insincere friends.
▶ **Cracked eggs** mean disappointment.
▶ **A nest full of eggs** suggests financial gain.
▶ **Eating eggs** means you will have a child soon.

Figs

Because of their appearance when split, figs are often associated with female eroticism – though in some cultures, they represent the male testicles. Either way, any fruit spilling with seeds is linked with libido and profit.

Fish

Because the fetus inhabits a watery womb, Jung believed that fish represented the unborn child, which can be generalized into a life force. Freud saw fish differently as symbolizing the genitals, and therefore the dreamer's attitude to sex.

Fruit

Fruits are a sign of sensuality, pregnancy and growth. Soft, succulent fruits such as a fig or a peach are associated with female sexual parts, long fruit such as bananas with the male member.

▶ **Green fruit** suggests disappointment and a need to work harder.

▶ **Rotten fruit** means family problems, missed chances and setbacks.

▶ **Collecting fruit** suggests a positive, optimistic attitude towards life.

▶ **Buying fruit** suggests an ordered, stable life.

▶ **Eating fruit** is associated with health and happiness.

▶ **Offering fruit to others** indicates generosity and prosperity.

▶ **Dreaming of fruit out of its season** used to be viewed as a sign of ill health, but this is now outmoded as most fruits are available just about all year round.

Grape

Grapes are associated with pleasure, sometimes to the point of decadence. This is partly because they are used to make wine. Through this link, to a Christian they can represent the blood of Christ.

Honey

This is a particularly powerful image of hard work and good health.

▶ **Eating honey** in your dream is a sign that represents independence.

▶ **Offering honey to others**, paradoxically, shows a shy nature.

Ice cream

Savouring an ice cream is one of the pleasures of childhood, so dreaming of it indicates pleasurable memories of that time.

▶ **If it tastes bad**, this suggests feeling disillusioned.

▶ **A melting ice cream** symbolizes inability to achieve your desires.

Jam

There's a link here with childhood pleasure, but the sticky nature of jam can also suggest difficult situations. Because it is usually red, jam can also represent blood, with possible associations with menstruation, losing virginity, and fear of violence.

▶ **Dreaming of making jam**, like baking, suggests a happy home life.

Jelly

Jelly is often children's party food, so it can symbolize childhood pleasure and perhaps relationships. Its lack of shape can indicate concerns about one's own identity and being influenced by others.

Lemon

The sour taste of lemons indicates bitterness and arguments.

▶ **Eating or sucking on a lemon** suggests a need for healing.

▶ **Cutting lemons** indicates anger and frustration.

Meals

Meals are usually identified with the pleasure of company, especially within the family, suggesting harmonious relationships.

▶ **If the meal is uncomfortably silent**, lack of communication is clearly an issue.

good to know

Still hungry?
Not feeling satisfied by food in a dream suggests that you feel starved of love and care. If the food was cooked or served by others, they are the focus for your feelings of neglect. If you prepared the food yourself, there may be issues about your sense of independence and whether you are looking after yourself properly (perhaps emotionally or physically).

▶ **Eating alone** suggests (positively) independence, or (more negatively) social isolation and lack of interest in life.

Milk

We get milk from our mother, so it symbolizes maternal instinct, kindness and nourishment. It can also represent relationships with others.

▶ **Choking on milk** suggests feeling smothered by a female in your life.

▶ **Spilt milk** indicates disappointment and indecisiveness.

Meat

Meat is often linked with financial dealing, with an element of hunting or seeking to gratify a need. A vegetarian will obviously see meat as a symbol of something unwanted. As it is flesh, meat is also identified with carnal desire.

▶ **Raw meat** suggests you see obstacles ahead.

▶ **Cooked meat** means achieving a target.

▶ **Eating large quantities of meat** indicates stress.

▶ **Ham** seems to be a particularly evocative meat. First, of course, the Jewish and Islamic faiths see it as unclean, and more generally as an image of not belonging, imagery shared in this case by vegetarians. To others, it can symbolize the pleasures of childhood family meals. However, some dream interpreters associate ham with emotional problems and loss.

Mushroom

Mushrooms symbolize change and development. They can also suggest the dreamer can be too hasty and should slow down.

Nuts

Nuts symbolize success in overcoming business problems, by getting to the core of the difficulty. If you can't get through the shell, there is a major problem you are trying to combat.

Olive

The olive branch has long been a symbol of peace and reconciliation. Because they are pressed to make oil, olives also suggest successful change, perhaps conflict resolved.

Onion

The layers of this vegetable indicate that there is a complicated issue that will take lots of work to understand – perhaps a family secret. The layers may also relate to the dreamers' inner self. Onions are also identified with unhappiness, misunderstandings and envy.

Orange

▶ **Eating oranges** has long been seen as a sign of grief and anxiety, linked to wounds and dishonesty.

▶ **A basket of oranges** signifies that change is needed to avoid problems.

Oyster

Oysters as food are linked with sensuality and indulgence. In the nineteenth century, they were a good omen for marriages, with much love and many children. More recently, they have been identified with unnecessary expense.

Pie

A pie is a symbol of the fruition of hard work, suggesting a reward to come. We also like to have our fair share of the pie, and so may reveal a concern we are not getting what we deserve.

Pizza

The huge range of pizza toppings suggests abundance and choices to make. It is also made from bread, so some of that material's symbolism may apply. The round shape suggests maternal feelings.

Potato

Potatoes are identified with financial problems. Fields full of them unharvested suggests uncertainty about the future. Potatoes often seem to be negatively linked with feelings of laziness or neglect.

▶ **Mashed potato** is a childhood comfort food, so take the dreamer back to that time or feelings associated with it. If the mash is lumpy and/or tasteless, there may be a link with school memories.

Rice

Rice is a staple food, so it is linked to happiness in the home. Grains of rice are associated with prosperity and friendship, and also, because of the fact that rice is thrown at weddings, with fertility.

Salt

Salt is a preservative, stopping rotting and corruption, so there are suggestions of purification, protection and dependability here.

▶ **Spilt salt** is traditionally bad luck, indicating a social embarrassment.

Soup

This is a warming, nourishing food that we closely identify with the love of our home and family. It is also perceived as strengthening, so there may be a feeling that you need to become more assertive.

▶ **Spilt soup** suggests social insecurity.

▶ **A pot of soup** represents your love and care for others.

Spaghetti

Spaghetti looks like hair, especially pubic hair, so there may be some erotic symbolism here.

Strawberry

This fruit delights the senses, signifying temptation and desire, and with strong links to female sexuality.

Sweets

Sweets represent pleasure in childhood, and are consequently often a symbol of love.

Tea

Tea is suggestive of home life, perhaps an indication that your work life is stressed and you long for the relaxation of home.

Tomato

The tomato signifies happiness and harmony at home.

Vegetables

Vegetables are a basic need, so dreaming of them is about your nourishment, whether that be intellectual, spiritual or material.

▶ **Healthy and abundant vegetables** indicate happiness and warmth.

▶ **Dried and withered vegetables** suggest sadness.

▶ **If the vegetable is phallic**, like a carrot or cucumber, there is a sexual element to the dream.

Watermelon

The shape and inner colour of watermelons suggest lust and passion. It is also very common for women who are pregnant or about to menstruate to dream about watermelons.

Wine

We identify wine with celebrating and companionship.

▶ **Drinking alone** signifies loneliness and depression.

▶ **Breaking wine bottles** in your dream suggests some kind of over-indulgence.

<aside>

good to know

Self-denial
Refusing food or not eating implies that the dreamer is concerned about food issues, possibly a worry about having an eating disorder or dieting. There is also a suggestion here of deliberate lack of fulfilment, perhaps spiritually (fasting has many associations with religion).

</aside>

Dream diary

To help you get started recording your dreams, use the dream diary pages that are printed on pages 97–112. Read the notes below first and there are some additional hints and tips overleaf.

Negative feelings
The most commonly reported emotions in dreams are fear, anxiety and anger. These and other negative feelings, such as sadness, occur far more frequently than pleasant sentiments, indicating that dreams have a valuable role as a safety valve for pent-up emotions.

Dream notes

Use the left-hand column for initially collecting information and impressions using the prompts that are provided.

Main action or event

▶ Write the key thing that happened, the main focus of action.

Who else was there?

▶ Do you know them? If you don't, they'll symbolize some part of your make-up.
▶ Could they be an archetype?

What was my role?

▶ Were you actively involved or passively watching?
▶ How would you describe your behaviour?
▶ Did you talk?
▶ Did you move?

Key objects

▶ What things were in the dream?
▶ Were any of them out of the ordinary or in the wrong place (this makes it more likely they symbolized something else)?

Feelings/fears

Feelings are intensified in dreams and many dreams address our hidden fears, so note down anything particularly useful here.

Other details

This is space for you to put in further information.
▶ What was the location?
▶ What colours or numbers did you see?
▶ Can you think of any puns that suggest you could understand the dream better using word play?

Links with my life

Note down any associations between your dream and your waking life.
▶ Did you recognize any people or places?
▶ Do you do any of the actions you witnessed.
▶ Did you behave how you always do in such situations?

Title

Giving a dream a title helps to clarify what it was about by identifying the key issues.

Possible meanings/links

Use the right-hand column to note down any possible meanings for parts of your dream. Use the guidance in this book and your own understanding of symbolism. For example, a sleek car might be associated with status and sense of identity, travel, your own journey through life. Don't be afraid to record more than one possible meaning if it occurs to you.

If you are really uncomfortable with putting things down on paper, try recording your thoughts into a dictation machine.

Interpreting your dreams

Once you have filled in the diary, think through the dream and imagine you are telling its story briefly to someone else. Some people find it helpful to have a friend to do this with – but be prepared for the inevitable loss of privacy as they prod around in your subconscious! Talking about your dreams with a trusted friend can provide another layer of understanding, because we tend to clarify our thoughts as we speak, and your friend may have valuable insights to make as well.

Keep recording your dreams to help you spot themes and links between them. Make any changes you find useful to the format of the diary so that it works for you.

---

must know

Interpreting your dreams

▶ Before writing anything down, go over the dream in your mind first.

▶ Don't get out of bed and move as little as possible.

▶ Record the dream as soon as you can, even if it is the middle of the night.

▶ Write down any dialogue first – it is the first thing that gets forgotten.

▶ If writing is too much of a chore, use notes, or draw.

▶ Write as briefly as possible.

▶ Consider any puns that would reveal the meaning through word play.

Date: Time:

Dream notes	Possible meanings/links
Main action or event	
Who else was there?	
What was my role?	
Key objects	
Feelings/fears	
Other details	
Links with my life	
Title	

Date: Time:

Dream notes	Possible meanings/links
Main action or event	
Who else was there?	
What was my role?	
Key objects	
Feelings/fears	
Other details	
Links with my life	
Title	

Date: Time:

Dream notes	Possible meanings/links
Main action or event	
Who else was there?	
What was my role?	
Key objects	
Feelings/fears	
Other details	
Links with my life	
Title	

Date: Time:

Dream notes	Possible meanings/links
Main action or event	
Who else was there?	
What was my role?	
Key objects	
Feelings/fears	
Other details	
Links with my life	
Title	

Date: Time:

Dream notes	Possible meanings/links
Main action or event	
Who else was there?	
What was my role?	
Key objects	
Feelings/fears	
Other details	
Links with my life	
Title	

Date: Time:

Dream notes	Possible meanings/links
Main action or event	
Who else was there?	
What was my role?	
Key objects	
Feelings/fears	
Other details	
Links with my life	
Title	

Date: Time:

Dream notes	Possible meanings/links
Main action or event	
Who else was there?	
What was my role?	
Key objects	
Feelings/fears	
Other details	
Links with my life	
Title	

Date: Time:

Dream notes	Possible meanings/links
Main action or event	
Who else was there?	
What was my role?	
Key objects	
Feelings/fears	
Other details	
Links with my life	
Title	

Date: Time:

Dream notes	Possible meanings/links
Main action or event	
Who else was there?	
What was my role?	
Key objects	
Feelings/fears	
Other details	
Links with my life	
Title	

Date: Time:

Dream notes	Possible meanings/links
Main action or event	
Who else was there?	
What was my role?	
Key objects	
Feelings/fears	
Other details	
Links with my life	
Title	

Date: Time:

Dream notes	Possible meanings/links
Main action or event	
Who else was there?	
What was my role?	
Key objects	
Feelings/fears	
Other details	
Links with my life	
Title	

Date: Time:

Dream notes	Possible meanings/links
Main action or event	
Who else was there?	
What was my role?	
Key objects	
Feelings/fears	
Other details	
Links with my life	
Title	

Date: Time:

Dream notes	Possible meanings/links
Main action or event	
Who else was there?	
What was my role?	
Key objects	
Feelings/fears	
Other details	
Links with my life	
Title	

Date: Time: Time:

Dream notes	Possible meanings/links
Main action or event	
Who else was there?	
What was my role?	
Key objects	
Feelings/fears	
Other details	
Links with my life	
Title	

Date: Time:

Dream notes	Possible meanings/links
Main action or event	
Who else was there?	
What was my role?	
Key objects	
Feelings/fears	
Other details	
Links with my life	
Title	

Date: Time:

Dream notes	Possible meanings/links
Main action or event	
Who else was there?	
What was my role?	
Key objects	
Feelings/fears	
Other details	
Links with my life	
Title	

Houses and buildings

We decorate our homes to show our character, and likewise, in dreams, the houses we see reflect ourselves. Consider whether you know the house in your dreams, or whether it is a new creation (see Homes and houses on page 118).

(see Homes and houses on page 118)

---

must know

Houses and buildings in dreams

▶ Remember that if you are familiar with the house in your dream, then the building itself has little significance: it is merely the background.

▶ However, a house that is created in your dream is central to its meaning. The overall condition of the house is significant as it reveals how we feel about our progress in life so far. Each room and object has a different symbolism attached to it, mostly related to facets of our personality.

Apartment

Much depends on whether you live or have lived in an apartment or flat. If so, then the setting relates to feelings or people in that place. If not, an apartment represents only part of the total house or self. The state of its decoration may illustrate your own outlook and current prospect. Because a flat is cut off from other homes, you may be avoiding certain relationships or rivals.

Attic

Attics have a number of meanings. First, being the highest room of the house, they represent the intellect and aspirations. Second, they are (usually) seldom visited hiding place for secrets. These could either be memories (generally happy ones) or repressed thoughts.

▶ **A tidy, well-lit attic** suggests an ordered mind and clear aspirations.

▶ **Clutter, darkness and dirt** indicate your thoughts are less organized and more changeable.

Balcony

Balconies are separate from the rest of the house but usually offer a wide view. Therefore they symbolize taking a step away from everyday life and perhaps getting a new perspective. Being high up, they can also indicate status. Balconies can also represent female breasts, so being on one may indicate a desire to be mothered.

▶ **Falling from a balcony** clearly reverses this status, and is linked to poor business dealings.

Basement

The basement represents intuition and the unconscious mind. A tidy basement suggests the dreamer is feeling satisfied. Mess indicates confusion and feelings of inadequacy. Unhappy memories are often 'stored' in the basement, such a dream may be indicative of associations with guilt or trauma.

Bathroom

This relates to cleaning yourself, possibly emotionally, maybe in the sense of releasing some thought or feeling.

▶ **Being unable to find the bathroom** suggests problems in expressing emotion.

▶ **A warm and cosy bathroom** may also suggest the womb, indicating thoughts about motherhood.

Bedroom

Bedrooms are private retreats. This room could symbolize the keeping of family secrets. Beds appear in dreams very frequently. They represent security and the private elements of relationships such as times of intimacy, sickness and rest. Consider carefully the state of the bed and how it relates to your life. Sometimes the bed can be interpreted more widely as encapsulating your life so far, as in the phrase 'You've made your bed, now you lie on it'.

▶ **Empty bedrooms** can symbolize death.

Carpet

Carpets are linked with wealth and ambition. A rich, luxurious carpet suggests prosperity, while a threadbare one indicates hard times.

▶ **Bare floorboards** were once linked with lack of money, but are now so popular the meaning is almost reversed, provided the floor is in good condition.

▶ **Weaving a carpet** suggests hard graft.

Cellar See Basement.

Corridors and hallways

Corridors are anonymous places that lead us somewhere. If we feel trapped in one, perhaps because it is endless, we are expressing frustration at never achieving what we want. The dreamer stuck in a corridor or hallway is in limbo, getting nowhere, perhaps trying to make a connection. Hallways can be anxious places, marking a change from the private to the public, so the dream may relate to a worry on this theme. As a kind of holding area, the hallway can represent pregnancy.

Cupboard

Anything where objects are stored suggests things being hidden away, such as memories and secrets. Consider whether the doors are open or closed, and the size of the furniture in proportion to other objects. There is also the well-known saying 'Coming out of the closet' to reveal hidden sexuality.

Door

Doors are openings, suggesting change, new opportunities, and entering something (which indicates a possible sexual element). A door opening out is more indicative of new experiences than one that opens in, which shows a desire for self-discovery.

▶ **Closed or locked doors** symbolize keeping something private and hidden.

► **Back doors** are more private than front doors, so indicate a link with private, perhaps family issues.

► **Front doors** are about public relationships.

► **Side doors** suggest evasion.

Fence

Fences are barriers, so in dreams they represent the obstacles in your way, which could, of course, be coming from within. The fence could be a warning that you are becoming introverted, and closed in, or it may be protecting you – you will need to consider the whole context of the dream. Fences are where boundaries meet, so the dream could be about sharing ideas and negotiating differences, or dealing with social barriers.

► **Falling from a fence** suggests you feel out of your depth.

► **Animals jumping a fence** into an enclosed area indicate you have help available to you somewhere. If they escape, the meaning is reversed.

► **A fence made of stretched wire** may indicate tension.

► **Building a fence** suggests that you are creating a barrier around you for protection.

► **Climbing a fence** indicates a rise in status.

Flat See Apartment.

Floor

The floor represents your foundation, the things that keep you stable, so an uneven or sloping floor indicates a fundamental concern. Consider what is above and below the floor in the dream.

Garage

Be clear about how you perceive your garage. Is it a storeroom? If so, does it hold garbage (unwanted thoughts and feelings) or does it protect your prized car (ambition)? Is it a retreat from domestic hassle where you can be idle or can think, or is it your route to the outside world? Now you can consider its significance in your dream. Opening the door obviously lets out whatever is in there, and shutting it closes the contents off again.

Garden

The garden represents how happy we are at the time of the dream, and our imagination. The state of a garden in our dreams reflects how much we feel we have grown as a person.

▶ **Green grass** suggests successful enterprise, while grass in poor condition denotes problems.

▶ **A vegetable garden** symbolizes prosperity and diligence.

▶ **A bare garden** with weeds indicates lack of spiritual growth.

▶ **An overgrown garden** suggests a lack of direction in your life, perhaps due to poor communication.

Gate

Like doorways, gates are thresholds to change. Judge from the rest of your dream whether the gate opens onto an exciting new opportunity or a kind of hell. What did the path through it look like? Obviously an open gate is more inviting than a closed one. Gateways can represent stages in life as we take on more responsibilities such as adolescence, marriage and parenthood.

Homes and houses

Refer to the introduction to this section if the house is your home (page 114). Our home personifies how we see ourselves, and our relationship with our family. It signifies your own feelings of security and self-knowledge.

▶ **Your home being broken into** shows feelings of being violated, or that you have not acknowledged some aspect of yourself.

▶ **Cleaning your home** signifies a search for self-improvement.

▶ **Visiting your childhood home** indicates some unresolved issues from that period, possibly relating closely to your own personal development.

▶ **If the house belongs to someone you know,** the dream is about your relationship with them.

▶ **If the house is created in the dream,** it relates to you, how you see yourself, and your body. For example, the ground floor is your lower body, the attic your head, and so on.

▶ **An old and run down house** suggests you are stuck in the past.

▶ **A crowded house** indicates the need for personal change.

▶ **Damage to the house** refers to your own perceived character faults.

▶ **Repairs** suggest personal growth.

▶ **Watching your partner** enter another house shows you subconsciously believe they are in a relationship elsewhere.

Kitchen

The kitchen is the heart of most homes, the centre of affection and where everybody interacts.

▶ **Untidy kitchens** suggest family tension.

▶ **People eating in the kitchen** is a sign of harmony and health.

▶ **A burning kitchen** indicates concern about a problem in family life (it used to foretell the death of the cook!).

Living room

The living room sets your social image to outsiders: it is your public face, as well as being an important part of your home.

▶ **An untidy living room** suggests that you feel you do not show your best side to others.

Roof

This represents protection from harm, including our own ways of dealing with problems.

▶ **Repairing a roof** suggests that you are finding new strategies for coping with stress.

▶ **A leaking roof** indicates a need for new ways to be found to handle difficulties.

Rooms

It is quite common to dream of finding a new room in your home. This depicts a new aspect of your own personality or a new situation.

▶ **A dark, threatening room** suggests repression.

▶ **If the room is pleasant,** you are feeling satisfied with your life.

▶ **A large room** represents the great potential you know you have.

▶ **A doorless room** is like a womb, so reflects your attitude to pregnancy or to your mother as a nurturer.

Stairs

Dreaming about stairs is quite common, especially among children. This may be because parents ensure they train young children to take great care on stairs, so they loom large in our unconscious as an image of danger, and tend to symbolize fear and lack of confidence.

▶ **Going up stairs** shows you are moving towards a higher level of understanding and/or achievement. You are also moving away from your baser urges.

▶ **Running up stairs** is often associated with the positive feelings of exhilaration and release.

▶ **Stumbling up stairs** suggests you will overcome problems.

▶ **Travelling down stairs** is a journey towards your unconscious, and perhaps a trip through some past difficulties. Running fast down stairs is a skill that children learn, so represents an achievement we are proud of – where something dangerous becomes a source of pleasure. So, for example, someone who conquers their fear of water and learns to swim well may dream of zooming safely down stairs at speed.

▶ **Winding stairs** indicate new, exciting developments.

▶ **Being pushed down stairs** shows a distrust of someone who is close to you.

Toilet

Toilets symbolize letting go of emotions or things you now see as not needed. This is a very private place, so it can also represent your need for your own space. Toilets also signify acceptance of natural functions and feelings. A blocked toilet suggests pent-up emotion.

Wall

Walls, like fences (see page 117), show that there are boundaries, but walls suggest more substantial obstacles to be faced, or a greater need for security.

▶ **A crumbling wall** shows you can rise above your problems.

▶ **Smashing a wall** symbolizes overcoming your own limitations.

▶ **Hiding by a wall** indicates shame.

▶ **Climbing the wall** shows that you are attempting to overcome the problem.

Window

'Window of opportunity' is a common phrase that suggests a meaning for windows in dreams, in that they indicate how receptive you are to new ideas. However, it may indicate a feeling of being under observation and a need for privacy.

▶ **Closed windows** reveal a feeling of being alone.

▶ **Broken windows** suggest you feel someone has been disloyal.

▶ **An open window** represents a new chance.

▶ **Peering out of a window** suggests too much interest in others, at the expense of your personal growth.

Insects

Insects generally represent problems in dreams. There may be something 'bugging' you, a 'pestering' worry that won't go away. Being like an insect in a dream is linked to feelings of insignificance and low self-esteem. More positively, insects can represent being alert and quick to respond to problems.

must know

Insects in dreams
▶ Stinging insects such as wasps, bees and hornets can stand for hurtful, stinging remarks.
▶ Parasitical beasts such as leeches, mosquitoes and ticks reveal a feeling that someone is benefiting from your work or good nature – or that you are doing this to someone else.
▶ Dead insects are thought to represent a dead foetus.

Ant

Ants embody the work ethic: they cooperate and never tire. So a positive interpretation would be that they show great teamwork. However, few people would be proud to be compared to an ant, and so they can represent feelings of insignificance, and of being lost in social conformity where you have no control.
▶ **Being stung by an ant** illustrates the small irritations of life.

Bee

As with ants, bees are seen as diligent and productive, but when flying they are also free and independent. Perhaps because of their ability to produce golden honey, bees have long been seen as a sign of future prosperity. A bee can sting, causing hurt to others, and dying in the act, so they can represent hurt, irritation and self-sacrifice.
▶ **A beehive** represents some sort of well-organized collective activity.
▶ **Bumblebees** are associated with anxiety.

Beetle

Beetles are associated with dirt and destructiveness, so have negative connotations. The suggestion here is that you sense your values and beliefs are under attack, possibly in quite an underhand way.

Butterfly

With their constant flitting movement, butterflies remind us of the need to settle in one place for a while, or with one person. This is a message to avoid shallow, superficial contact with ideas or people. They are also the end result of a transformation from being a caterpillar, and so symbolize the beauty of creativity.

Caterpillar

A caterpillar is at the start of a process that will see a major transformation, so in dreams it represents the need to keep developing and growing. Gardeners may sympathize more with the older interpretation that caterpillars are a sign of bad luck.

Cockroach

The presence of cockroaches in a dream indicates your subconscious need to change your attitude to life. Killing these unwelcome creatures suggests that you will feel able to make the changes needed.

▶ **Flying cockroaches** suggest a journey.

▶ **Cockroaches on a wall** indicate family arguments.

Flea

The presence of a flea or fly suggests that someone or something is annoying you and has been doing so relentlessly for some time. The more insects there are, the bigger the problem. The fly can also represent someone who looks very busy all the time, but actually achieves very little.

▶ **Being bitten by fleas** implies gossip about you.

Fly See Flea.

Grasshopper

These have been seen as bad omens for centuries, perhaps because they threaten crops and so livelihoods.

Leech

This is a powerful metaphor for something draining you of energy. The 'something' could be other people, or your own feelings or actions. Being covered in leeches implies self-disgust.

Lice

The presence of lice or any other parasite in a dream is a sign of worry and guilt about selfishness, either in the dreamer's behaviour or those around them, who are 'feeding' off him or her.

Maggot

Maggots are closely identified with death, because of their feeding habits. There may be a problem 'eating away' at you, or the maggot may represent someone behaving parasitically.

Mosquito

The mosquito sucks our blood, or life force, and so in a dream is a symbol for something that is sapping you of energy. There is also a suggestion of feeling under attack here.

Moth

The moth living in stored clothes suggests a festering dispute that needs to be aired and resolved. Another image associated with moths is that of flying into a flame, suggesting feelings of self-destructiveness.

Scarab

The ancient Egyptians believed scarab beetles protected them in the afterlife, so this is a message about your attitude to death and ageing.

Scorpion

The scorpion is a menacing sight, with a prominent sting. Its presence in a dream indicates feeling hurt and even fearful. Scorpions can also represent death and rebirth. There is a theme of destruction and negativity in this image. If you take an interest in astrological signs, the creature could represent someone born under the sign of 'Scorpio' in your life.

Spider

Much depends here on your attitude towards spiders, and what the spider does in the dream. If, like many people, you are frightened of them, then they represent something you fear. This is really common – one survey found that more than a third of people who had a nightmare involving some sort of beast said it had a spider in it. However, spiders also tend to symbolize female power.

▶ **A spider spinning a web** becomes a symbol of creativity and perseverance.

▶ **If you become trapped in a web,** you are feeling entangled in some way in your life, perhaps in a relationship with a woman – this is especially true if the spider bites you. That said, spiders are generally taken to signify good luck and protection, unless you kill them.

Wasp

Not surprisingly, wasps are seen as a bad sign in a dream, representing anger, possibly that of someone behind your back who envies you.

▶ **A wasp's nest in your roof** (which symbolizes your aspirations) suggests obstacles in your way.

Worm

Worms represent death and decay, destroying affection and threatening financial problems. In dreams, the worms may symbolize your enemies, or your own low feelings of self-worth. A worm crawling on your body is feeding off your generosity.

Life, death and the spiritual

This section deals with dreams about new life, life stages such as marriage and death, and spiritual and religious elements such as God. Dreams about death are not necessarily negative: they can be concerned with transition and letting go of the past – giving up smoking, for example.

Abortion

This represents stopping the development of something you were bringing into your life, like some new business venture or relationship. It is most likely to relate to a love affair (imagined or real) that left you with feelings of guilt or damage.

Ageing

Ageing in a dream is often identified with wisdom and forgiveness. You may also be pondering your own mortality.

Angel See page 148.

Bible

The Bible represents truth, moral standards and belief. Much depends on how you regard the Bible in your waking life. It may symbolize your own beliefs, or that of religious people or organizations. There is a suggestion that you are seeking some kind of inspiration or comfort.

Birth

Assuming the dreamer is not about to become a parent (or keen to), a birth dream signifies a new beginning of some kind, or a plea from the subconscious to release the child within you. Women have this dream more than men, and it is generally symbolic of new relationships or insights. If men have this dream, it is more likely to relate to new business or creative ventures.

Giving birth to a baby with defects is a common anxiety dream for pregnant women, and for others, a signal of anxiety about some project. The more extreme version involves producing some kind of monster, which is a sign of frustrated creativity. Some psychologists argue that dreaming of a birth is a way of addressing issues to do with our own birth and subsequent experiences. The idea of rebirth can apply to many aspects of your personality, and can be represented in many ways: coming out from some isolated place or a cave, for example. Women who are not pregnant may dream of giving birth as a reminder of their own female characteristics.

Blessings

We all seek recognition and affirmation from others, and the act of being blessed has been an important part of human culture for thousands of years. So it is no surprise that blessing is a regular phenomenon in dreams. The act of blessing is an act of resolution and forgiveness that we often crave.

▶ **Receiving a blessing** from someone who is loved but not demonstrative in our waking life helps to make the dreamer feel complete.

▶ **Seeking a blessing** from another indicates feelings of inferiority.

▶ **Blessing another** in a dream is a way of giving encouragement and showing power.

Burial

Burial is part of letting go of something, so a burial dream may have no link with death at all. You may be burying a memory, a relationship, or some aspect of yourself. This may be a positive or negative thing – being reconciled to something you have struggled to accept, or trying to hide it (in which case you might dream of burying something alive). Of course, by burying something from the past you are also commencing a new stage in your life, so this could be a dream of rebirth.

Cemetery

Cemeteries are not exactly joyful locations, so going to one in a dream suggests grief, sadness and possibly depression. However, since a cemetery houses dead things, it could be the place where the dreamer gets rid of unwanted parts of their life, such as a bad relationship or an unwanted trait. Another view held by some interpreters is that cemeteries are not necessarily eerie or unhappy in a dream, but represent the next stage in our existence: a rebirth.

▶ **If you feel happy in the cemetery,** this suggests coming to terms with a problem and being able to overcome difficulties.

Church See page 167.

Coffin

This may, of course, be a symbol of your own death, or of the end of a relationship – for example, if you see the person involved in the coffin. In these cases, everything hinges on what is in the coffin. However, many dream interpreters see the coffin as a symbol of feeling confined in some way. The coffin could also represent the womb, suggesting a need for security and peace.

Cross

This is obviously a powerful Christian symbol, but it has more general connotations with enduring pain and suffering. As a religious sign, it stands for healing, reconciliation and judgement. To a devout Christian, this is a comforting sign, suggesting inner healing and renewal. If you are avoiding the cross in the dream, you may be trying to avoid being judged for your actions. The cross might also suggest that you are feeling hardship in your waking life. This shape can also show an answer is wrong (as opposed to a tick).

Dead people

A dead person appearing in your dream indicates that you have unresolved feelings about them, or about what they mean to you. When someone dies we have to adapt to seeing them as a memory rather than as part of our waking lives, and dreams can help to achieve this. If they died long ago, it is more likely that the circumstances of your current life have an echo with something in theirs, from which you are trying to learn. You may be trying to take on some of their characteristics, which you admired. They may also represent something that you now need to leave behind, to allow to wither and die.

Death

For an introduction to dreaming of death, see the common dreams box to the right.

▶ **Dreaming your own death** is a way of being reconciled with mortality and of recognizing your own achievements or lack of them. Some people emerge from such a dream grieving for themselves, others feel empowered and content.

▶ **The death of someone you know** is another upsetting dream, which may indicate the end of a relationship, or a need to remove that person (or what they symbolize) from your life. You may simply be concerned about their health.

▶ **The death of a stranger** of the opposite gender will most likely be linked to your anima or animus (see The Anima and Animus archetype box on page 156), which is the female or male part of your psyche. Even if the unknown person is of the same sex as you, they will represent some element of your personality.

▶ **Hanging** was regarded by Freud as a symbol of male castration, so suggests sexual insecurity. Death by guillotine has similar meanings.

Devil

The Devil is evil, so to a religious person will represent an opponent of God. However, the Devil has a much wider significance to many people, being identified with temptation (especially sexual), cruelty and anger. So the Devil can represent the negative thoughts we are all capable of, that we have perhaps guiltily tried to repress. He can also be the emblem of fear – particularly of illness.

▶ **Demons** work for the Devil spreading distress, so their meanings can be similar, but they are less powerful than the Devil and could stand for your shadow self: your negative aspects that you try to keep under control.

Disease

Unresolved issues or painful memories can appear in dreams in the form of a disease, illness or infection. If there is something that is 'eating away' at you, such as some kind of unfinished business or an inability to deal with some problem, this is more likely to be manifested as an infection. Illness symbolizes low confidence and depression.

▶ **Curing diseases** is a sign that you want the good that you do to be recognized and to influence others.

▶ **If a disease is identified with a particular person**, you are unhappy about their role in your life.

(See also the section on Bodies and body parts, pages 56–63.)

Ghost

There are a number of interpretations for seeing a ghost (see also Dead people). Ghosts are generally associated with guilt and memories of past traumas. You may be feeling isolated within your world, so the dream is suggesting that you change in some way. The ghost can represent some repressed thoughts that you are beginning to confront, especially if you reach towards it in the dream. In such cases, the ghost is likely to be demonic. Since children often fear ghosts, the dream may be taking you back to something in your childhood.

God

As usual, much depends on the dreamer's attitude to who is in their dream. A deeply religious person will see God as a divine presence, the ultimate in perfection, to be worshipped and obeyed. Many spiritual people will view God as a symbol of perfection, and consequently a reminder that they can only strive for perfection, prompting feelings of repentance for their sins.

▶ **If God is viewed as a controlling force,** His presence in a dream allows the dreamer to escape responsibility for their actions.

▶ **If God speaks to you,** you are likely to be feeling guilty and in need of redemption.

▶ **Seeing ancient mythological gods,** such as those of the Greeks, Romans or Egyptians, should lead you to consider their specific role and its symbolism for you.

▶ **Dreaming you are God** suggests feelings of superiority.

Grave

This could symbolize something that is not 'on the surface', rather, it is in your unconscious.

▶ **Dreaming of digging a grave** suggests lack of confidence in a new project.

(See also Cemetery.)

Heaven

We may not all believe it exists, but we all understand the idea of heaven as a peaceful, happy place full of hope.

▶ **Dreaming of heaven** suggests your wish to feel positive and energized and to get away from your current troubles.

Hell

We tend to identify hell with problems we have made for ourselves, and with our own fears. Therefore it can become a projection of how we see ourselves, so if we feel horrible, hell will look horrible. Dreaming of hell will show you your unhappiest memories, your failed relationships and your inner anxieties.

Illness and infection See Disease.

Jesus Christ

The interpretation of the presence of Christ in a dream depends, as so often, on the dreamer's view of Him. He may simply be a source of spiritual sustenance and a reminder of the suffering some endure. The figure of Christ is a tremendously powerful symbol of life, love, suffering and salvation. However, Christ can also be seen in dreams as a reminder of the great mystery of who we are and why we were born. Some interpreters also see Christ as a symbol of the positive aspects of the dreamer's personality: a reminder of the good that is in all of us.

Marriage

The dream is most likely to be about a real or desired wedding. However, it could be about balance. Since most dreams are about ourselves, the union may be between different aspects of yourself to create a happier, more harmonious 'you'. Weddings also mark changes in our lives as we move on, so the dream may relate to some joint venture. You may be dwelling on your own commitment to relationships and a lessening of independence, symbolized by the wedding – look at the whole context of the wedding.

Murder

This clearly shows hostility, but your victim may represent some aspect of yourself that you view negatively and wish to be rid of, particularly if the victim is a stranger. So you could be dreaming of ending an addiction. This is such an extreme dream it suggests that you are under great stress and have been repressing anger. However, it is worth noting that as society continues to struggle with and debate the issues of assisted suicide and euthanasia, this dream may simply reflect a situation in your life. (See also Suicide.)

Pregnancy

If you are pregnant, the dream will reflect your own feelings and concerns about this. Pregnancy is also clearly a symbol for growth and development, and will often be about an idea that you have not expressed openly.

▶ **A baby dying inside you** represents the failure of some project. (See also Birth.)

Saint

We identify saints and other holy figures with spiritual enlightenment, so their presence in a dream indicates a quest for fulfilment in this area. There may be a moral element to the dream, suggesting that you are not comfortable with choices you have made and feel you may be judged as lacking morality.

Suicide

This may appear at first as a completely negative dream, and if you are harbouring thoughts of suicide, you should seek professional help. However, this dream can have positive aspects: you may be killing off a part of yourself that you no longer need, such as an addiction or a trait you dislike. In this sense, the suicide dream is therefore about your development as a person who is comfortable with yourself. Seeing a stranger commit suicide will also relate to some aspect of your own character, which makes you angry.

Objects

Any number of objects can appear in a dream, and once you ignore any that simply contribute to the setting, all involved in the action will have a symbolic meaning. This section also includes natural objects, from the acorn, below, to the Jungian archetypes of the sun, moon and stars.

must know

Objects in dreams
▶ Consider the location of the object (was it where you would expect to see it?) and any variations in colour and shape that may add to its meaning.
▶ Ask yourself whether the object was being used in a natural way, and who it belonged to.
▶ Finally, consider whether it has any special significance personal to you – a childhood toy, something you are frightened of.

Acorn

This is a well-known symbol of growth from small beginnings, so it has been seen as an omen of wealth and happiness for centuries.

Ambulance

We identify ambulances with emergency, fear and injury. You may be worried about your health. If the ambulance has many wounded people in it, they represent your emotional wounds and bad experiences, and the dream is a subconscious sign of fear of letting go of these and moving on. (See also Accident on page 70.)

Arrow

We aim arrows at targets, so they represent our ability to achieve goals. A broken arrow reveals worries about not reaching the target, but can also suggest the end of a relationship. Freudians draw sexual meaning from arrows, as they are long and straight and penetrate things.

Bag

A bag can carry your hopes and ideas in it.
▶ **Heavy bags** show we feel overburdened.

▶ **Empty bags** are a positive sign of a desire to go out and achieve more.

▶ **A handbag** is a symbol of a woman's identity.

▶ **A sleeping bag** is a sexual symbol, and can also represent the womb.

Balloon

Much depends here on the state of the balloon. Colourful big party balloons are linked with celebration and achievement. However, as they are only full of air and can pop any second, there is an inherent fear that 'the balloon will burst'. Furthermore, as they deflate, balloons come to represent failed projects or relationships, and their final bedraggled state is like that of a condom.

▶ **Releasing a balloon** suggests letting go of something.

Blanket

Blankets give us warmth and security. Perhaps you are seeking protection, suggesting a lack of affection in your life. You may be 'wrapped up' in some feeling or experience – check the significance of its colour.

Book

We gain knowledge and wisdom from books, so much depends on the nature of the book in the dream. It may be suggesting a new direction or skill for you. Books can also represent the imagination and escape from everyday reality.

▶ **A dusty, old book** indicates some forgotten information from your past.

Bottle

Because we store liquids in bottles, in dreams they hold repressed emotions. They also symbolize the vagina.

▶ **If the bottle holds alcohol** like beer or wine, it suggests a time for winding down and socializing.

▶ **An empty bottle** indicates lack of inner strength.

Box

As somewhere to store things, the box represents memories and things you are holding back. Its location in the house may be important (for example, attics have different meanings to basements) – see the Houses section (pages 114–21). Did you open the box? If not, why not? The contents of the box are likely to secrets, perhaps fears, and the box itself suggests limitation and feeling 'boxed in'. If you are familiar with mythical stories, you may be thinking of Pandora's box, which released evil into the world but also a small symbol of hope.

Cage

Things in cages are powerless, which may be how you're feeling.

▶ **If you are in a cage,** you are feeling inhibited by social pressures or by repressed feelings.

▶ **If you place something such as an animal in a cage,** you are controlling it and what it symbolizes.

▶ **A bird in a cage** indicates frustration at being unable to express hopes.

Camera

Cameras hold memories, so much depends on what you are taking a photograph of. If it is a person, you are trying to hold on to them, which suggests you feel they are moving away from you in some way. Cameras also stop the action and allow you to study it, so you could be feeling rushed and unable to understand everything that is going on around you. (See also Picture.)

Candle

We tend to identify candles with mystery and romance, but depending on the circumstances of the dream they can also represent a search for something, because they shed light. Candles are phallic in shape, so there may be a sexual association. If such as candle is unlit, there are fears of impotence or sexual rejection.

▶ **If someone else is holding the candle**, they may be leading you towards something.

Cigarette

Much depends here on your attitude to smoking. If you are happily addicted, they represent pleasure and social interaction (if you smoke with others). Other people might view them as a symbol of disease and death, or of being 'cool'. The phallic shape lends itself to sexual interpretation, especially oral sex.

▶ **Stubbing out a cigarette** suggests the end of a relationship.

Clock

These clearly show time passing (or running out), suggesting that the dreamer is feeling rushed and stressed by a deadline. We also link ticking clocks with heartbeats, which may tie in with feelings of mortality, or with emotions (feelings of the heart).

▶ **A stopped clock** denotes death (perhaps the death of an emotion).

▶ **Hands moving backwards** indicate a lack of progress in your life.

Clothing

Clothes set our public image: how we want to be seen – our confidence and status.

▶ **Losing clothes** indicates feeling vulnerable.

▶ **Clothes being praised or criticized** indicates your self-esteem.

▶ **Buying clothes** suggests positive change by the dreamer – but consider what the clothes were, as they might be providing protection, for example.

▶ **Dirty or shabby clothes** imply bad habits and low self-esteem.

▶ **Constantly changing clothes** suggests indecisiveness.

▶ **Tight clothes** show you feel restricted or inhibited in some way.

▶ **Unbuttoning** implies you are opening up in some way, and doing up buttons means the opposite.

(See also Shoe and must know box on page 138.)

Dress sense

Apron: Maternity.

Belt: Social manners, restriction.

Blouse or shirt: Emotions, public image.

Coat: Public image, protectiveness and secrecy.

Dress: Femininity.

Fur: Pubic hair, the womb.

Gloves: Avoiding 'dirty business', trying to be pure.

Hat: If not identified with a specific role or group (like the police), protection. Hats also symbolize our thoughts, so changing hats shows a new decision. Tall hats show power and authority.

Raincoat: How you deal with emotions.

Skirt: Femininity, sexuality.

Socks: Personal qualities and standards.

Suit: Work, public image.

Trousers: Masculinity.

Underclothes: Sexual intimacy, inner feelings, secrets.

Uniforms: Being part of a group, authority.

Computer

These signify access to knowledge, and communication. They also have strong connotations with work and office life. Freudians find sexual meaning in the many buttons, slots and disks that we need to manipulate. Depending on how you view computers, they can represent opportunity or coldness and lack of feeling.

▶ **A computer you cannot control** shows anxiety about work and technology.

Crown

A crown is obviously a symbol of high status, suggesting recognition for achievements and feelings of superiority.

▶ **If you are holding on to the crown**, you fear you could lose this high status.

Dish

Dishes represent ideas. A dish of food suggests the immediacy of these ideas – you want to do them now.

▶ **Leftover food** means outdated ideas that can be jettisoned from your life.

▶ **Unwashed dishes** show dissatisfaction with how your life is going.

▶ **Washing dishes** shows getting ready to move on.

Doll

Dolls represent girlhood to women, and, more generally, childhood and relationships with parents.

▶ **Caring for the doll** represents love and nurturing.

▶ **If you become the doll in the dream**, you are trying to avoid being held responsible for your actions.

Feathers

Feathers carry the meaning of the bird that they came from, so if you can identify the bird, look in the Birds section on pages 52–5. Feathers may also suggest flying (see page 175) or phallic symbols.

Flag

Of course, flags are designed to represent countries, so the dream may relate to this. Flags also represent pride and community.

▶ **Burned or mistreated flags** show anger directed at some aspect of that country.

Flowers

Flowers represent kindness and compassion – so try to recall if the flowers were healthy or in need of attention. The parts of a flower can be associated with our sexual organs, and so more generally with fertility. Some interpreters see plants as standing in for your children if you are estranged from them. Plants can also suggest a season for the dream.

▶ **Withered or dead flowers** suggest disappointment and the death of feelings.

(See also must know box above and Colours on pages 66–8.)

Furniture

As the house represents our life, so furniture is our attitudes and habits. Chairs reveal the dreamer's or sitter's attitude.

▶ **A large, cosy chair** suggests someone who is at ease with the situation.

▶ **A small, uncomfortable chair** shows the opposite, especially if it is set away from the others.

must know

Flower power
Clover: Happiness and harmony.
Cornflower: Contemplation.
Daisy: Childhood, female sexuality.
Ivy: An invasive presence in your life.
Lotus/Water lily: The Ancient Egyptian symbol of creation, seen by Buddhists as a symbol for spiritual development.
Orchid: Fertility.
Red rose: Romance.
Sunflower: Adaptability.
White flowers: In certain cultures these are associated with death.

must know

Glittering dreams
These jewels have a special significance:
Amethyst: Healing.
Diamonds: This is the hardest, most valuable stone. It can be identified with greed, or something that will be long lasting.
Emerald: Spiritual growth.
Opal: Fantasy.
Pearls: Treasure discovered, inner beauty.
Ruby: Wealth and power, leadership.
Sapphire: Peace and faith.
Topaz: Intuition.

A table symbolizes working with others. Its quality indicates how you feel about your relationships.

▶ **A bare table** suggests fear of poverty or loneliness.

▶ **A stained tablecloth** indicates feelings of guilt.

▶ **A table with broken objects** on it suggests arguments with friends or family.

▶ **A table with unusual objects** shows confusion.

Glass

Glass is an invisible barrier, suggesting an emotional block – so breaking glass may be a positive symbol. However, since broken glass can cut, there is a hint that you might be hurting others with comments or behaviour. (See also the must know box on drinking on page 86.)

Gun

A fairly obvious male sexual symbol, but also a powerful message of death and brutality. Explosive release of emotion.

Jewels

Jewels can show your sense of self-worth (how you 'treasure' yourself). Some pieces of jewellery will be identified with the time you got them or the giver. Jewellery embodies materialistic values, especially for men. For some, the jewellery will represent their lack of respect for material values. Much depends, of course, on how you get the jewellery: was it purchased, found, a gift or stolen? (See also the must know box above and Ring.)

Key

A key is a symbol of having access to something, or being able to close it off: it all depends what door the key opens. So you are either trying to find something out, or making it secret. There is also clearly a possible sexual meaning here, too.

► **Finding keys** suggests that you have solved a problem.

► **A bunch of keys** represents feeling or taking responsibility for something.

Ladder

A ladder takes you to a specific place, so it represents your progress towards your goal. You are headed for a new opportunity, or increased awareness of something, perhaps linked to a change of perspective.

► **Rising up** may be a spiritual or social journey.

► **Going down** the ladder suggests moving away from these things.

► **The rungs** represent your path, and missing rungs indicate obstacles.

Lamp or torch

Anything that casts light offers guidanceto the dreamer in a search for greater awareness. Turning it off (or a broken light) shuts out the things that might be able to help you.

Letter

Clearly this reveals information, but first consider your usual attitude to mail: when the post arrives, do you dread the arrival of bills, or relish the thought of news from friends? This will be reflected in your dream. Letters often signal enlightenment, understanding and opportunities.

► **Unopened letters** show something being repressed or ignored.

Mask

Masks conceal and show different roles.

► **Seeing others in them** suggests you do not fully trust them.

► **If you are wearing a mask,** you may be playing a role.

Money

Money is identified with status and power and, for some, personal value. In a dream, money may represent what is valuable to you – which may not be cash at all. It can stand for opportunities in life.

▶ **Dreaming of not having money** suggests issues about ambition and self-esteem.

▶ **Giving money** in a dream is linked with seeking love and attention.

Moon

The moon is a feminine symbol of serenity and hope – in many cultures it is viewed as a mother figure. The moon is also associated with mystery and intuition (and madness – the meaning of lunar).

▶ **A full moon** suggests completion.

▶ **A new moon** symbolizes new beginnings.

Musical instrument

These show your capacity to express yourself creatively. Playing an instrument also suggests a desire for harmony and balance. An out of tune instrument indicates that adjustments are needed to achieve this. Instruments also have many possibilities for interpretation as parts of our sexual organs. Heavy beats and drumming may link with the rhythms of sex.

Nails

Hammering in nails represents hard work, but nails bond things together, so they are a symbol of unity through working together. Nails also stand for punishment and suffering because of their use in the crucifixion. There is also the possibility of them standing for male sexuality.

Needles

Needles and pins both have sexual connotations because they penetrate. You may be 'looking for a needle in a haystack' – seeking something very hard to locate.

▶ **If the needles are used for mending,** there may represent a relationship that needs repairing.

Newspaper

We use newspapers to gain insights, so maybe the dream is helping you to shed light on an issue. Perhaps you want to be in the newspaper, so you are seeking attention or recognition.

Paper

We write and read ideas on paper, so anything written on it in a dream will be significant.

▶ **A blank sheet** can show a dearth of ideas.

▶ **Crumpled paper** suggests rejection.

Picture

What is in the picture? It is likely to be highly symbolic.

▶ **If you are drawing it**, you are creating that image.

▶ **If you are hanging it**, you are accepting it.

▶ **If the picture is only in black and white**, your subconscious is asking for more excitement in your life.

▶ **A blurry image** suggests fading memory or an attempt to hide what is really happening.

   (See also Camera.)

Radio

Radios in dreams allow our imagination to suggest what people are saying about something – which is really a way to give the subconscious a voice. If there is lots of interference, you are having difficulty expressing yourself in your waking life, maybe because you haven't thought things through clearly yet.

Ring

In many cultures, a ring is a symbol of commitment, which could be to a relationship or a project. It also shows how true you are to your promises.

▶ **A broken or missing ring** shows mistrust or lack of faith in your ability to keep to a commitment. This can apply equally well if the ring is not on your finger.

▶ **If the ring is a gift or an heirloom**, it symbolizes the relationship with the giver.

A ring is also a circle, a symbol of completion (see Circle on page 68).

Rock and stone

Rock represents stability, suggesting you feel on solid foundations in your life. So, for example, your relationship is 'solid as a rock'. Rocks and stones are permanent, suggesting unchanging attitudes. These could be a strength, like moral certitude, or a weakness, like inflexible obstinacy. Sometimes stones can carry magical meanings.

▶ **If you are trying to climb over the rocks**, they symbolize the obstacles you have to face.

Rope

Ropes tie things together, so they represent some sort of hold. If you are tied by them, something is holding you back in your waking life.

▶ **Climbing up a rope** suggests determination to achieve something.

▶ **Climbing down** shows disappointment.

▶ **Tightrope walking** suggests risk and lack of stability – but with a goal at the end of it.

Rubbish

We throw out rubbish, so it represents things you want to be rid of, which could include unwanted characteristics or habits.

▶ **Clearing out someone else's garbage** suggests that you are helping them clear their reputation.

Shoe

Shoes connect us to the ground, so they represent your whole approach to life and feeling 'grounded'.

▶ **Changing shoes** indicates a change in your role.

▶ **Wearing the wrong shoes** shows you are not comfortable with the direction you are going in. If they are a certain type of shoe, you want to gain the characteristics of whoever would wear them.

▶ **Losing your shoes** reveals you are searching for your own identity.

▶ **Being barefoot** can suggest letting go of responsibilities, or getting in touch with nature and your basic instincts.

Soap

This suggests you have something to wash away, indicating feelings of guilt.

▶ **Cleaning yourself** can bring a sense of wellbeing.

Star

Stars can represent insights into your own dark unconscious. We link stars with dreams that we wish to follow, indicating a desire for a new location or position in life.

Sun

The Sun is the source of creation and insight – it was the key god for the Egyptians. It symbolizes life energy, enlightenment and, through this, peace of mind. The Sun is a Jungian archetype described by the psychologist as, 'the classical symbol for the unity and divinity of the self; source of life and the ultimate wholeness of man.'

▶ **Sunrise** suggests new beginnings.

▶ **Sunset** indicates closure.

Sword

Anger and social power (because of its symbolic use by authority figures).

Telephone

Telephones obviously represent communication, but with people who you cannot get close to, even in a dream. So they are remote from you in some way. The message is, of course, from your own subconscious, and may be an attempt to make you face something you have been avoiding.

▶ **If you just let the phone ring,** you are blocking something out.

▶ **If you are making an unanswered call,** you are struggling to reach someone or some idea.

▶ **An emergency call** suggests a crisis.

must know

Tool box
▶ **Drills** penetrate hard surfaces, suggesting resistance to your efforts.
▶ **Hammers** show strong willpower, almost aggression, often led by a moral judgement.
▶ **Saws** change the shape of things, so can indicate new attitudes. They also cut through, suggesting insights and getting to the key point.
▶ **Screwdrivers** finish off the job, and make sure things stay in place, so they can represent creating stability.

Television

If you dream yourself on television (assuming you have no yearning for fame), you are communicating something that you feel unable to express directly, so it could be a powerful message. You are watching the 'news' from your subconscious. An alternative is that you feel your views are not getting the attention they deserve, so you need to broadcast them more widely or powerfully.

Ticket

Tickets represent opportunities. If you have bought the ticket, this suggests that you feel you have earned the chance that is coming up. So a ticket reveals your confidence in what you are doing.

Tools

Tools are used to make things, showing self-expression and creativity, or to repair, revealing that there is damage that needs fixing. So your dream could be showing that you need to be more imaginative in using your skills, or directing you towards a problem. You may not be surprised to learn that Freud associated tools with the penis and intercourse.

Tree

Trees represent the growth of your inner self. Consider which season the tree is in as this could be significant.
▶ **The top of a tree** is high up, showing aspirations.
▶ **A healthy tree** shows emotional strength.

- ► **A neglected tree** suggests low self-esteem.
- ► **Roots** are the foundations (representations of family background, culture).
- ► **Trunks** show how energy is directed (into growth, thought, emotion).
- ► **Branches** are your own capabilities, and members of your family.
- ► **Leaves** are the living growing parts of you, and the results of your efforts.

Umbrella

This is a device to protect you from your unconscious, and in this case it is stopping water (which symbolizes life and emotions) from reaching you. So umbrellas reveal an unwillingness to face our feelings or traumas – an attempt to escape reality. If there is a sexual element to the dream, an open umbrella represents female sexuality, while a closed one becomes phallic.

Weapon

Weapons show the need for protection or wishing to hurt others, which implies conflict and fear. Assuming you do not know the attacker or victim, they will have a symbolic value, which is clearly crucial. The more powerful the weapon, the greater the frustration that is being released. Consider how the weapon is being used, and in what context. For example, a weapon coming out of someone's mouth shows the impact of the words they are uttering. Most weapons are also phallic symbols. (See also Violence on page 79.)

(See also Violence on page 79.)

---

must know

Trees and the Bible
A dream of Nebuchadnezzar the King of Babylon, who died in 562 bc, is reported in the *Book of Daniel*. He saw a lovely tree with green leaves providing shelter for birds in its foliage and beasts in its shade. Then a messenger from Heaven ordered the tree to be cut down and the King to be chained to the stump, where he was left to feed on the grass like an animal. Nebuchadnezzar sent for Daniel, an expert on dreams, who told him that the tree represented royal power and glory. When it was cut down, he became nothing but a beast, living off the grass. Daniel's interpretation was that the King should accept the heavenly power above him, just as he was above the beasts in the field.

People and characters

Most dreams have people in them. If you recognize them, the dream is about unresolved issues in your relationship with them, or what they represent, which will be some characteristic you admire or feel dominated by.

---

must know

People in dreams

▶ Seeing people from your past indicates that some present element of your life has echoes of how you felt with them – so, as usual in dreams, the dream is about yourself, not them.

▶ Unknown people in your dreams suggests an encounter with your anima or animus (see the box on page 156).

▶ Some jobs have a symbolic role. For example, workmen solve problems. Police and other authority figures represent power (see the Powerful people box on page 159).

▶ There is a big difference between seeing people and being them in a dream. If you are seeing them, who is in control of the situation? If it is not you, you are carrying feelings of being dominated and need to be more independent.

▶ Sometimes a person in a dream will embody certain eternal characteristics (such as courage with superheroes). These are known as archetypes (see the box on Jungian archetypes on page 28).

Actor/Actress

Seeing an actor indicates that you want (or need) to play a role and receive attention for it. Alternatively, you may already be 'acting' by presenting a false façade to people and your dream is recognizing this. If the actor is famous, you are probably keen to acquire some of his or her traits.

Alien

Aliens represent aspects of yourself that you or others have not come to terms with. This could be something deep within, or an attitude you are trying to accept. If there has been a major change in your life, such as a new home, job or relationship, you may be feeling lost and in a different world. It is also possible that the alien represents an attempt to escape reality.

▶ **A dream of alien abduction** suggests a fear that you will become distant from your family and home. You are feeling threatened.

Angel

Angels appear in dreams quite frequently. The interpretation depends, of course, on how you view them. A deeply religious person will see an angel as God's messenger. Someone who believes in prophecies may hold with the idea that angels announce births or deaths of those close to you. For all of us, angels symbolize love, goodness and protection, so they are welcome visitors – but they are there because something is troubling you, so study the rest of your dream carefully. Try to recall how much dialogue you had with the angel. If they are acting as a messenger, they will not talk much, but if they were acting as a sort of spiritual adviser, more conversation is inevitable. The presence of an angel in a dream implies that the dreamer is seeking help, and does not know where to find it in the waking world. (See also Nurses.)

Architect

Architects design new buildings, so in a dream they represent the desire for change and fresh challenges. If it is clear what kind of building they are working on, look up that building in the Places section on pages 164–71.

Artist

Artists are obviously creative people, but they are also allowed to be irrational in a way that others are not, so your dream may suggest a need to follow your instinct rather than your intellect. The picture they are working on may represent a scene from your life.

▶ **If you are sculpting,** you may feel there is a deep problem you have to 'get to the core of'.

Baby

While we identify babies with innocence and new life, in dreams they are more likely to represent the baby in us: our vulnerability and need for attention, traits that we tend to try to disguise in real life. So a poorly or crying baby indicates a need to be nurtured, or a wish to avoid responsibility. If you are pregnant or hoping to be, the meaning of your dreams is less likely to be symbolic and just shows your understandable concerns and preoccupations.

▶ **A starving baby** suggests dependence on others.

▶ **A tiny baby** indicates your fear of weaknesses being spotted.

▶ **A dead baby** stands for the end of some part of your life.

▶ **An adult with a baby's head** suggests you feel immature.

▶ **A fetus** indicates your desire to regress to somewhere comfortable with no responsibilities.

▶ **Happy babies** show you feel emotionally stable.

▶ **Forgetting a baby** suggests you are trying to hide your weaknesses.

Bailiff

The presence of a bailiff in a dream clearly shows anxiety about your finances, but there is also a hint here that standards of ethical or business practice may be low – you are questioning your own integrity.

Ballerina

A ballerina is beautiful and moves gracefully without apparent effort. Your dream is about living up to the idea of beauty, and how you are coping with life's obstacle course. The precise interpretation depends on the behaviour of the ballerina.

Boyfriend/Girlfriend

The presence of a boyfriend/girlfriend obviously shows you are thinking about this relationship.

▶ **Dreaming he/she is dead** suggests something in you or the relationship is 'dead'.

▶ **Discovering infidelity or that he/she is gay** indicates your own insecurities.

▶ **A dream involving an ex-boyfriend/girlfriend** shows

there are unresolved issues from that relationship, or, more generally, the hopes that you had nurtured at that time.

Brother See Family members.

Bus driver

Bus drivers lead a group on their journey, but ultimately simply travel the same circular route. They can therefore represent a kind of progress, yet there are doubts here about whether the project will actually get anywhere at all.

Butcher

Obviously a food provider, but also a bloodied bringer of death, the butcher can symbolize aggression, but also sacrifice of some kind. (See also Blood.)

Child

This could refer to your own childhood, the childlike feelings you have sometimes, or to feelings of dependence. Maybe you just want to go back to a time of greater freedom and less responsibility. Children usually express themselves without inhibition, so consider what they said and whether you would secretly like to do this too.

▶ **Dreaming of your own children**, or of having your own children, simply links with this relationship or wish. If you dream of your own children being younger than they are now, you are feeling as if you are needed less than you were.

▶ **Dreaming of being in charge of children** relates to your feelings about power, whether you have it and how effectively you are using it.

Celebrity
Dreaming of a celebrity indicates that you would like to acquire some of their personality traits or that you want to pursue a relationship with them. Think about what you most identify the celebrity with – if it is one main element (like being dominated by their father), that is what you could be dreaming about, applied to yourself.

▶ **Being a celebrity yourself** in a dream reveals a wish to achieve and be rewarded for it.

▶ **If someone you know becomes famous** in the dream, you are frightened of losing them, and perhaps doubt their loyalty to you.

must know

The Divine Child archetype
The Divine Child is a Jungian archetype (see the box on page 28) whose innocence and vulnerability warns the dreamer against self-importance and cynicism.

▶ **If you are the child in the dream**, you are powerless, and therefore the dream relates to an authority figure, perhaps a parent or boss.

Christ See Jesus Christ on page 132.

Crowd
Crowds show what you perceive to be the attitude of others towards you (indifferent? threatening?) and how you feel about others. Being lost in a crowd suggests lack of direction in life. If you were leading a crowd, consider how this happened: the way you led them was the central, important element that could direct you in the future.

Daughter See Family members.

Dentist
Dreaming of teeth is extremely common because they represent our public face. So dentists have an important dream role because they look after these important things. Much depends on your relationship with dentistry: do you associate it with pain, improvement, and the words you say? Dentists work above us and have the power to change how we look, and to men, can represent someone castrating them (because they remove parts of our body), so they may be representing a parent or authority figure. Women's dreams sometimes link tooth removal with childbirth, so again the dentist has a different, and powerful, symbolic role as obstetrician. (See also box – Teeth – on page 62.)

Doctor
Doctors tend to be authority figures, sometimes standing in for a parent in the role of giving guidance. They are also healers, so dreaming of doctors may indicate a wish or a need for some kind of treatment (not necessarily medical).

▶ **If you are the patient**, the dream suggests feelings of powerlessness and emotional unrest.

▶ **If you are receiving strange treatment**, or cannot understand the diagnosis offered, there is a communication problem in your life, which is frustrating you.

▶ **If you are the doctor in the dream**, it is reflecting a comforting, helpful role in your life, which you may feel you need to expand. Consider the complaint and the nature of the patient to discover more meaning.

Dwarf

Quite a lot of dreamers report seeing dwarves in their dreams, and the most common interpretation is that they represent part of your personality that has not developed fully, or that has been repressed. So the dwarf is like a message from your subconscious of an element of your character that wants to be expressed. Consider what the dwarf is doing, and whether you have a secret wish to do the same.

Family members

Family is important to most people so, of course, we are going to see them in dreams, even if we no longer see them every day. A dream involving some or all of your family could well be just that: a dream about you and your family. How you see each member in your dream suggests the state of your relationship with them. This can be influenced by what you see as their major characteristics, for example a family member who is most diffident and distant can represent your own feelings of isolation. The following suggestions explore what members of the family can represent symbolically:

▶ **A contented family group** suggests harmony and balance in your life.

▶ **Brothers and sisters** can symbolize friendship and rivalry, authority or vulnerability (depending on their age in relation to

must know

The Father archetype
A father is also a Jungian archetype (see the box on page 28) symbolizing male strength and authority, and every aspect of the role of a father. (See also the box for Old Man or Woman archetype on page 160.)

the dreamer). Brothers can also represent the masculine part of the dreamer, so dreaming of a feeling of anger towards them may be a sign of inner frustration.

▶ **Daughters** can represent your feminine side, emotional connection and also the state of their parents' marriage (because they are the result of their union). They can also stand for your own youth and embody your feelings about that time in your life.

▶ **Fathers** stand for authority and protection, which may be presented in a positive or a negative light. They can also symbolize conventional society and how it sees you.

▶ **Mothers** represent your capacity for caring, giving yourself, and your emotional life. In a sense they can represent the unconscious mind, while the father stands for the conscious mind and our actions.

▶ **Parents** represent the elements of both father and mother and how effectively they work together. So it can be argued that a dream involving your parents is not about them, but about the 'father' and 'mother' characteristics that are part of your personality. So a dream in which your parents are in harmony suggests that you feel you yourself are balanced and happy.

▶ **Sons** often represent our ambitions for the future.

▶ **Uncles and aunts** can represent how the dreamer actually feels about their father or mother.

▶ **Grandparents** symbolize love and wisdom.

Father See Family members and The father archetype box on page 153.

Fireman

Firemen represent protective masculinity and the need or wish to be rescued – a sort of hero figure, which can, of course, be you. Fire is hot and powerful, so a fireman can symbolize how we control our passions.

Ghost

Ghosts represent the things we fear or feel guilty about. Most ghost dreams can be traced back to childhood memories, often involving parents.

▶ **Dreaming of seeing the ghost of a dead friend or relative** indicates 'unfinished business' with that person: unresolved issues.

Giant

Children's stories are full of powerful, scary giants, so it is not surprising that they appear in dreams. The giant represents a major, dominating obstacle, which could just be one of your inner feelings.

▶ **If you become the giant in the dream,** you are trying to control other people.

Girlfriend See Boyfriend.

God See page 131.

Grandparent See Family members.

Hero/Heroine

Dreamers often feature as the hero of their own dream. This can be interpreted as a sign of confidence, in that you were able to act as a hero. Alternatively, you could be haunted by the fear that your weaknesses render you incapable of being a hero. The challenge facing the hero will most likely symbolize conquering some negative feeling in your own subconscious. As ever, consider the context of the dream so that you can decide what powers the hero used (would you like to develop similar skills?) and whether the opponents were people you know, which would suggest that you find it difficult to trust them.

must know

The Hero archetype
A hero can also be a Jungian archetype (see the box on page 28) of an inspirational role model. This noble figure is usually taken from classical mythology or popular culture (e.g. Superman). The Jungian hero is a positive image celebrating the skills we have gained and the progress we are making.

The Anima and Animus archetypes

Psychologist Carl Jung believed unknown men or women appearing in dreams of the opposite gender were archetypes (see page 28) with an important function in representing key latent traits of the other sex.

▶ **For men,** an 'anima' represents their caring side, showing emotions and trusting intuition.

▶ **For women,** the 'animus' represents dynamism and assertiveness.

In both cases, the make-up of the anima or animus will be dictated by the person's experience of and perception of the opposite gender, and how much he or she is already aware of his/her own 'male' or 'female' aspects. In dreams, these archetypes can help us fulfill our potential by guiding us towards characteristics that we may not have considered part of our self, helping us to gain greater skills and energies.

Intruder

If you have been burgled, this dream is most likely your way of releasing the fear it instilled in you. If not, the intruder represents your own guilt about how you have been behaving or thinking. The house is a symbol for your whole life, so breaking into it and damaging or removing things in it are clearly signs that you have done wrong to yourself.

Jury

Being part of a jury clearly symbolizes the need to make an important decision, carefully thought through. Being before a jury suggests you feel some kind of judgement will be made about you.

Lawyer

Meeting a lawyer in a dream shows you accept the need to take advice. This suggests there will be worries about some difficulty in your waking life. The lawyer may represent your own confidence in your own decision.

Lover

If a stranger becomes a lover in a dream, they represent the extremes of sexuality, and symbolize an ideal or an unwanted lover, depending on your feelings towards them.

Magician

A dream about magical qualities can often concern the dreamer's own subconscious. There may also be a feeling that you are being fooled about something – perhaps by yourself, or maybe by the superficial charm of someone you have met.

Man

▶ **If the man is known to you**, the dream is therefore about him.

▶ **If not,** the man probably represents a masculine part of you: rational, competitive, assertive characteristics.

▶ **If you are in conflict with the man,** these traits are dominating you, or you fear them.

▶ **An old man** in your dream stands for forgiveness or wisdom.

▶ **Women may dream of their ideal man,** or he may represent an assertive part of their personality.

▶ **A wild, ape-like man** represents our most basic, animal urges.

(See also the box on The Anima and Animus archetypes, opposite.)

good to know

The anima and animus in literature
In literature, the anima and animus can be seen in the characters of Adam and Eve, Antony and Cleopatra and Romeo and Juliet, and in dreams they can appear as very dominating, 'larger than life' people.

Master

Dreaming of being a master in charge of a group of people indicates a desire to be more assertive. It suggests feelings of inadequacy and that you need someone to lead you.

Matador

These signify courage (or the need for it), and a challenge you are facing. Given that they kill bulls, the dream may symbolize the death or absence of some basic drive.

Mother See Family members and the box on The Great Mother archetype on page 158.

Nun See Religious people.

must know

The Great Mother archetype
The Great Mother is a Jungian archetype (see the box on page 28) represented by the Virgin Mary, some other divine female or the dreamer's own mother. She represents our progress towards independence and mature love. As a giver of birth, she stands for the cycle of life: birth, death and regeneration. (See also the box on The Old Man or Woman archetype on page 160.

Nurse

Nurses are mother figures, indicating a need to be taken care of in some way.

▶ **A domineering nurse** or matron suggests rivalry with the dreamer's sister.

Nurses are often seen as angels, so refer also to that entry, and to the one for doctors.

Orphan

To be an orphan in a dream means that you quite likely feel rejected and abandoned. This feeling may refer to part of your character, or alternatively to some childhood memory.

Parent See Family members.

Passenger

Clearly a passenger is not in control of their journey so being one in a dream indicates a sense of frustration that others are making decisions for you.

▶ **If you are carrying the passengers**, you may be feeling exploited by lack of independence in others.

Police

If there is a member of the police force in your dream, you need to recall your emotional state at this point. They may represent protection, suggesting you need support in some area of your life.

▶ **If the police are chasing you,** your dream is about guilt, and a sense that you are not doing everything you should.

▶ **Policewomen** are more likely to represent some moral problem than policemen.

Referee

Referees indicate some kind of battle within yourself that you are trying to resolve, perhaps a choice or an outside influence.

Religious people

Dreaming of a spiritual leader such as a reverend or priest suggests that you are seeking the respect of your community, or guidance. Nuns represent abstinence and purity.

▶ **A woman dreaming of being a nun** is showing dissatisfaction with her life as it is.

Royalty

Royalty used to represent status and prosperity, but our view of royal institutions has shifted and today royal dreams are open to wider interpretation. Dreaming of becoming royal is still most likely a wish for wealth and power.

▶ **If you dream that you join royalty,** you are aspiring to social advancement because royalty stands at the pinnacle of society, representing social order.

▶ **Kings** are identified with fathers, power and feelings of superiority.

▶ **Princes** are have associations with masculine qualities (they can be the animus for a female – see the box on The Anima and Animus archetypes on page 156).

▶ **Princesses** can be an anima for a male (see the box on The Anima and Animus archetypes on page 156), or a kind and sympathetic nature.

▶ **Queens** represent mothers, convention and a desire for recognition.

did you know?

Powerful people
Powerful figures such as policemen, judges, soldiers and so on are all connected with the dreamer's own views of power and empowerment.

▶ If you are asserting the power, you are feeling in control of your life. Power dreams often follow a romantic conquest. The people you are commanding are symbolic of the elements of your own life that you wish to contain. Consider how you are applying your dominance: by example, by negotiation, manipulation? These indicate your own perceived strengths.

▶ If you are subject to someone else's power, there are feelings of lack of independence, inadequacy and frustration apparent.

must know

The Old Man or Woman archetype
These Jungian archetypes (see the box on page 28) represent wisdom, allowing the dreamer to grow through their own knowledge and experience. The man will be a father (also known as the Father archetype, see the box on page 153), teacher, priest or other authority figure. The woman (also known as the Great Mother, see the box on page 158) is the source of fertility and abundance.

Sailor

Sailors represent a wish to explore the unknown, including our own subconscious (which is often symbolized by water). They also have to cope with stormy seas, suggesting the dreamer is concerned about forthcoming emotional turmoil, or getting into 'deep water'.

Santa Claus

Santa Claus is, of course, an important childhood memory for many of us. In dreams he can represent a family time in the past, and a need to be more (for)giving. Children believe in Santa Claus, and learn over time not to, so there may be some symbolism here to do with your own (non-spiritual) beliefs.

Servant

▶ **If you are the servant in a dream,** there are underlying issues about social class, or feeling that you are being used.

▶ **If you have a servant working for you,** the suggestion is that you are over-dependent on others for help.

Sister See Family members.

Soldier

A soldier clearly represents conflict, which may include a desire to express your secret opinions.

▶ **If you are arguing or fighting with the soldier,** you have some internal conflict, or tension within your family.

▶ **If you are with the soldier,** you are coming to terms with some difficulty.

▶ **A dead soldier** indicates uncertainties.

▶ **A woman dreaming of a male soldier** may be feeling under threat from a relationship.

Son See Family members.

Spy

Dreaming of spies indicates a sense of suspicion about the motives and actions of others. This may relate to your business or emotional life. You may have discovered something you are not supposed to know and be suffering from guilt about it.

Stranger See The Shadow Stranger archetype, right.

Teacher

Teachers are authority figures but there is an obvious link here with knowledge and skills. You may feel you have something to learn that would be useful. The issues may be with authority and seeking approval, or with being made to feel as if you are the student.

▶ **If the teacher is known to you,** the dream could, of course, be about your dealings with them.

Thief

This suggests you are afraid that you will lose something that you have gained, possibly (if self-esteem is low) because you didn't deserve it anyway. (See also Intruder.)

Twins

In astrology, opposites are represented by twins. The opposites influencing your dream could be your

must know

The Shadow Stranger archetype
The Shadow Stranger is another of Carl Jung's archetypes (see the box on page 28). It can be any shape, it may be yourself, someone you know, a stranger or an animal, but it will have an unsettling, slightly sinister air. It may chase you, bully you, do bizarre things, or just lurk as an intimidating presence. The shadow represents the (perceived) negative aspects and weaknesses of our own character, things we might barely accept as part of our make-up. Its presence is a subconscious message to come to terms with this aspect of your personality.

The Trickster archetype

Tricksters such as clowns, fools, jesters and harlequins occur so commonly in dreams that psychologist Carl Jung included them in his group of archetypes (see the box on page 28). The trickster behaves wildly, is basic, self-centred and shows no sympathy for others. However, he carries no threat and can be a source of wisdom. The trickster's appearance in a dream suggests that the dreamer is feeling unsure and threatened, especially about social situations or relationships with siblings. He represents our potential to change, to transform ourselves by using our own inner strengths.

conscious and unconscious mind, or some conflicting emotions that are causing an imbalance in your psyche. The context of the dream will provide clues about the internal conflict you are suffering.

Uncle See Family members.

Victim
▶ **If you are the victim of someone or something in the dream,** you are feeling powerless and hurt in your waking life. This may be a mechanism for avoiding responsibility.
▶ **If you are victimizing others,** you may be feeling guilty about your behaviour, but it is possible that you are still expressing your own hurt and anger about damage received from others.

Waiter/Waitress
You are not meeting your own needs because you are spending so much time helping others. A more positive interpretation is that you are showing an awareness of the needs of others.

Werewolf
Werewolves are frightening and uncontrollable creatures that are sometimes disguised as normal people. The 'creature' they represent in your dream is some aspect of your life or personality that you are scared of, such as a violent, unpredictable temper.

Witch
Stories we hear in childhood often feature evil, magical and usually ugly witches. We identify witches with lack of care and being heartless, so this

has an echo with something in your life – possibly your feelings about your relationship with your mother. Witches represent power and evil. They can do good with their magic, so may not be evil, but magic is a short cut, an unnatural way of doing things, so you are feeling unsettled by the way someone is behaving. Perhaps the witch is encouraging you to use your own creativity and intuition to bring out the 'magic' in yourself.

Woman

An unknown woman in a dream symbolizes the traditional female qualities of nurture and being able to express emotions such as love. The woman may represent your mother, or female aspects of yourself. Depending on the dream, she may be a sign of temptation and guilt.

▶ **Old women** indicate wisdom and ageing. An old woman may be the dreamer's mother.

▶ **A pregnant woman** signifies some new beginning.

▶ **A female goddess** is a symbol of the dreamer's strongest or most desired characteristic.

▶ **Two women** suggest ambivalent feelings towards something.

(See also Sister and the Great Mother, Anima and Animus and Old Man or Woman archetype boxes on pages 158, 156 and 160.)

Zombie

As one of the living dead, a zombie represents total disconnection from your emotional life. You feel cut off from the real world, especially relationships: there is something you need to face.

Places

The places in dreams are the setting for the action, and they set the mood for the whole dream. For example, a cold or frozen setting indicates feelings of being left out, passionless. Big buildings mean big ideas. Buildings under construction mean plans and ideas.

must know

Places in dreams
► Anything that has no firm base, such as deserts or marshes, suggests a lack of emotional stability.
► An underground setting is linked with the subconscious mind.
► When a building appears in a dream, as usual think about what it means to you – you may have uncomfortable memories of swimming pools or courts, for example.
► Consider, too, the condition of the building that you see. Well-run, beautifully decorated buildings suggest pride and care. Dilapidated, run-down buildings encourage feelings of neglect and isolation. High places are indicative of aspirations and hopes.

Abroad

Being abroad indicates the dreamer wants his life to change in a major way, showing he feels unsettled. To identify what the country represents, consider your attitude towards it, and perceptions of the place. If you have any experience of that country, how would you describe it? Was it stimulating or depressing? Were you lonely or with a group of friends? The country may be symbolizing these feelings.
► **Someone of your opposite sex coming from abroad** suggests a desire for a new relationship, or a new kind of relationship.

Abyss

An abyss represents risk. Further interpretation depends on how you were feeling in the dream. If you were afraid of falling in, the abyss stands for your own private fears, of death, failure, relationships – you will know. It is most likely linked to a lack of confidence about some aspect of your personality. If you were not afraid, and just looking down, the abyss represents a challenge or obstacle in your life that you know you need to overcome. Your subconscious is telling you that you can succeed in this, and need to plan what to do.

Amusement park

To a child, these represent fun. To an adult, they can stand for fun in childhood, but adults also have anxieties about safety and fear of risk associated with amusement parks. This location is likely to represent your feelings about escaping everyday life and having more fun without responsibilities. If you fear a ride you go on in your dream, the meaning is similar to the anxieties represented by an abyss (see opposite).

Bank

These stand for finance, or your bank of resources. The dream is likely to concern your plans for the future and whether you can afford them. The plans need not be financial: they could involve emotional resources or your social network, for example. We also tend to identify banks as a place for negotiation and possibly confrontation.

Bar

This is a place for relaxing, possibly being irresponsible and consequently feeling guilty about it. To be in the bar or pub is to be away from your home, which in dreams represents your life to date. So this location represents escapism from the responsibilities of daily life. Bars can also be very male environments, so can symbolize male power.

Beach

We generally go to the beach with our family, so there may be associations with how you feel about family gatherings. On a more symbolic level, the beach is where earth and water meet, and there could be feelings about life processes such as life and death. The sand represents the rational mind, while water symbolizes emotions. The point where land becomes water represents a major change, where we might not feel as in control as we were – becoming 'all at sea'. So the location could stand for a change in your life, such as parenthood or retirement, in which the sand represents how far you have got already, while the water is symbolic of the journey to come.

▶ **Playing with sand in the dream** has a sense of time running out.

   (See also Sea and Water on pages 181 and 183.)

Bridge

Bridges connect, suggesting a change in circumstances and getting over a problem. Try to recall what was under the bridge in your dream, as this should make the meaning clearer. Bridges can also represent moving from the past to the future.

▶ **A damaged bridge** suggests a broken relationship or connection (as in 'you have burned your bridges'). The length of the bridge will suggest how much time and effort is required to make the connection.

▶ **'Building bridges'** is a phrase we use about overcoming difficulties, usually in communication.

Carnivals and circuses

▶ **Attending a strange carnival** and not being part of the events suggests a feeling of separation and discord – even deception.

▶ **To be participating** indicates you expect some exciting, unusual entertainment soon.

▶ **The need to escape** suggests lack of harmony at home.
We don't just identify the circus with childhood trips. In a circus we encounter fantasy, fear and courage, presented as an exciting spectacle. So dreaming of a circus combines strong, even passionate feelings with the idea of being watched. Go back over all the other elements in the dream for guidance.

▶ **An empty circus ring** could stand for feelings of missing out, or the prospect of excitement to come.

Castle

Castles are fortresses, keeping out attackers. So castles represent security and our own defence systems. The rest of the dream should tell you whether these are keeping you stable, or over-protecting.

▶ **A crumbling castle** indicates your lack of faith in your defence systems. They are also very much a remnant of the past, so the dream may concern your own history.

▶ **A castle under your command** suggests that you particularly like to be in total control.

Cemetery

These are obviously related to death, but they are the resting place of the dead, so the associations tend to be with a new stage in the life cycle, a sense of moving on towards stability. This location can also suggest thoughts of things in your life that you have buried away, perhaps ideas or past relationships.

▶ **Dreaming of sleeping in a cemetery** indicates you are comfortable with the notion of death.

(See also Life and death section on pages 129–30.)

Church

Like any religious building, churches represent organized religion and our feelings towards it. Depending on your attitude to church, they can also stand for the local community and its opinions of you, morality, spiritual belief, feeling blessed and the cycle of life. Obviously the events of the dream are crucial here – a wedding dream is very different to one of a funeral. With their towers and gateways (openings), there is also a lot of potential sexual symbolism in church structures, so these buildings can represent how we feel about all aspects of union, including intimacies.

City

A city represents a combination of work, opportunity and our relationship with the rest of society.

▶ **If you dream of your own city** or one you have lived in, the dream will relate to your past.

▶ **A strange city** suggests change.

▶ **Being alone or lost in a city** indicates feelings of isolation and anonymity.

▶ **A ruined city** shows worry about financial or legal issues.

Cliff

This represents some kind of risk about which you must take a decision. It may be, for example, that the cliff represents a major barrier to your plans and aspirations.

did you know?

Men's vs women's dreams
Research indicates that men's dreams are more often set outside, somewhere the dreamer knows, while the location for a woman's dream is more likely to be indoors, but similarly in a familiar location.

Countryside

A lush, green setting that is vibrant with flowers and trees sets a positive tone for a dream, suggesting a very healthy emotional state. However, bare sections, or piles of rubbish, detract from this and suggest lack of passion, or grim reality, invading your thoughts. Forests represent your natural, inner feelings, including your subconscious. In stories, forests are often places for magic and battles between strange forces, so their presence in a dream indicates a willingness to explore and experience new things, and a powerful imagination. Being lost in a forest stands for fear of the unknown and a need for direction in your life. Valleys are associated with fertility and therefore with growth and development.

▶ **A valley without plant life** in it suggests loneliness.

Court

This is obviously a place of judgement and may indicate the dreamer's fears that they have been dishonest. Otherwise, there may be legal issues preoccupying their mind.

Desert

These are lonely places full of hardship, and so carry unhappy associations with lack of creativity and all kinds of barrenness. In the Bible, people go into the desert or the wilderness seeking a sense of direction and new meaning. The sand shows lack of security in life. If you reach an oasis, this is a haven from the hardships of the world – unless it turns out to be a mirage! If you are looking for an oasis, you are seeking to escape pressure in your life.

Hairdresser

A barber or hairdressers is a place where we change our image, so you may be pondering altering your own appearance. A haircut is something done to you, so there may be an element of not feeling in total control here, too, which makes it a dream about anxiety and outside influences.

Hospital

Clearly this suggests a concern about health, but the symbolism may extend to healing the body or the mind. It is common for people receiving therapy to dream of this location.

Island

Islands are not easy to reach, so an island represents isolation, being in a rut and unable to find a way out of it. Of course, sometimes we escape to islands as a refuge where we can relax, so consider the overall context of the dream. Maybe you are trying to avoid confrontation?

Jungle

We see jungles as remote, unexplored places in which to have adventures, suggesting a desire for excitement and discovery. They can also be dangerous locations where we get tangled up, and so in dreams they can represent fears of getting caught up in some problem you can't control.

Labyrinth

This is a sign of complex problems that will take a lot of effort to solve. You may find they can be resolved by intuition (suggested by green plants and trees) or you may realize that you need to ask for help. Sometimes a maze can represent the tangled path of your life, and walking through it is a way of coming to terms with unresolved conflicts you have been through.

Library

Libraries store knowledge, so their presence in a dream indicates you feel a need to research something before continuing with a project. They are also fairly sterile spaces so could suggest feeling out of touch with your feelings.

Lift

This links with recent ups and downs, such as a change in status, prosperity or security. Much, of course, depends on the direction the lift takes.

▶ **Being trapped in one** suggests frustration and feeling restricted in what you are allowed to do.

Mansion

This may suggest a need for more room (perhaps figuratively, in a relationship that is in a rut). Mansions also stand for grandeur and power, and the dream may show your desire for higher status.

Maze See Labyrinth.

Monastery

This type of building is a place of serenity and spirituality where there is calm acceptance of the challenges life throws up. They tend to be seen as communities. If the dreamer is part of it, they feel accepted, if not, they are feeling socially isolated.

Mountains

Mountains symbolize the path you must take to achieve your ambitions: so there is the prospect of advancement, but also the presence of obstacles. Consider the context of the whole dream to decide whether the mountain is a sign of your aspirations or of what is blocking them. Height in dreams is associated with improved understanding, so climbing up the mountain shows you are making progress. Mountains often represent the lack of confidence the dreamer has in himself.

Palace

Palaces represent a privileged lifestyle – and perhaps a warning against being too regal and pretentious. Palaces can also represent potential that needs to be fulfilled, or grand ideas that you want to implement.

Prison

This is obviously a place of punishment, where right and wrong is recognized.
▶ **Being in a prison cell** suggests feeling repressed, a lack of opportunity.
▶ **Seeing something or someone in the cell** indicates your resentment towards them.

Pub See Bar.

Pyramid

These symbolic buildings now represent ancient knowledge and ingenuity, and a striving for higher consciousness. They are also associated with death.

School

This represents the chance to start a new life and learn fresh skills, unless the school is one you attended, when you are trying to resolve some conflict encountered there. All educational institutions represent learning in dreams: you may need certain information, or be seeking advice.

Theatre

Unless the dreamer has some professional role in the theatre, dreaming of being in one suggests a feeling of unreality, people playing a part.

▶ **If you are on stage**, you feel you may need to play a role to deal with some difficulty. It also indicates discomfort at being in the public eye.

▶ **Watching the stage** and you are watching elements of your personality.

Underground

Like the basement in a house, the underground is home to our subconscious. Being underground shows you have a hidden side, or traits that are repressed. There may also be a desire for greater security in life, or a wish to remove yourself from daily life.

Volcanoes

These are linked with ejection of long repressed material from underground – your subconscious. There are associations with feelings of emotional release and clearance – and an obvious sexual metaphor for ejaculation.

Zoo

A zoo is a place where natural things are held behind bars. The natural things will be your own basic urges and instincts, possibly to do with sexuality or relationships. These are being repressed, and the state of the animals you see will suggest how you feel about this. (See also the section on Animals on pages 42–51.)

Travelling

We are all on a journey through our lives, and travel in our dreams represents part of this trip and how we feel about it. Sometimes the destination may just be an idle wish rather than something symbolic, especially if it is a place of leisure. If there is no destination, maybe you feel your life is going nowhere.

must know

Travelling in dreams
▶ Consider whether the journey is a familiar one or not.
▶ Work out how well or badly the trip was going and who or what you met or saw on the way.
▶ All will contribute to the meaning of the dream. For example, braking indicates (obviously!) a need to slow down, suggesting you feel out of control.
▶ Dreaming you are in a hurry on a journey suggests feelings of stress and lack of preparation.
▶ Consider, too, whether your dreams are usually based around your life or a way of escaping elements of it.

Airplane

Airplanes appear very frequently in dreams. They represent change (or a need for it), a move into the unknown, and the height they travel at suggests freedom and a higher consciousness. So a plane stuck on the ground reveals a sense of frustration and lack of progress.

▶ **A plane crashing** indicates you fear you have been over-ambitious (which may simply reflect lack of confidence). Some women dream of plane crashes as a metaphor for rape. Some interpreters believe that planes can also represent a part of your journey through life (including your emotional development). So dreams of crashes are references to disturbing and upsetting events in your past.

Freud saw the shape of a plane as a phallic symbol, indicating a link with a sexual journey. To him, a plane crashing suggests a fear of impotency.

▶ **A plane having difficulty in landing** suggests concerns about carrying out plans, and of not being in control.

▶ **Planes being attacked** indicate some worry about criticism.

▶ **Switching planes** reinforces the message of change and new direction.

▶ **A plane hijack** shows unresolved issues from your subconscious, and a feeling of not being in control.

Airport

These clearly represent a starting point for, or a connection to, a new part of your life: a wish for change.

▶ **If you get on a plane,** you feel confident about this new venture.

▶ **If you don't get on a plane,** your doubts are holding you back.

▶ **An empty airport** suggests a feeling of lack of support from others, which is possibly delaying your plans.

▶ **A busy airport** suggests ambition and support from others.

Bicycle

Think back to when you learned to ride a bike: it is probably the earliest achievement you can remember accomplishing. So a bicycle can symbolize your own personal motivation to get something done, or learn a skill. The dream may also be taking you back to a stage in your life when a bicycle was important, perhaps as a much-wanted present (showing a desire for recognition) or as your means of transport (standing for independence). Riding a bike requires confidence and balance, so these ideas may be part of the dream meaning – especially if you fall off it.

must know

Car part symbols
▶ **Problems with the accelerator** indicate difficulties with your own drive and energy.
▶ **Problems with the brakes** suggest anxiety about controlling your life.
▶ **The steering wheel** represents your ability to make decisions.
▶ **Headlights** show the way, so they represent your ability to see ahead and gain insights.
▶ **The boot** of the car carries your luggage: memories.

common dreams

Flying

To interpret a flying dream, consider whether you felt you were flying towards or away from something: was it a positive or a negative journey? We associate flying with freedom, empowerment, the ability to gain perspective and overcome obstacles. It can be argued that flying dreams see us trying to escape from restrictions and rules. Others believe that by flying above others we assert our dominance over them. For more, see main entry, opposite.

Bridge See page 166.

Car

Dreaming of being in a car is a very common part of many dreams. The car can symbolize a number of things. Consider the overall context of the dream and, if appropriate, the events in your life. Cars are an indicator of achievement and status in our daily lives, so the make of car, if it is not your own vehicle, may be relevant. We also achieve greater independence when we learn to drive (just as we did at an earlier age when we began to ride bicycles). So the car, like the bicycle, can represent independence or that period in life when it was celebrated. Journeys in dreams generally symbolize our journey through life, so the car represents our own drive and control, our decisiveness and ambition. So consider how easy or difficult the route was: this is your journey through life. Is it an uphill struggle or a series of scary, tight bends full of alarming surprises? How did you deal with the 'traffic' of your life?

▶ **If the dream includes a journey you recognize,** consider the symbolism of the destination. Alternatively, your subconscious may be warning you of dangers on that route – maybe you habitually forget to check the road at some point, and this is worrying you.

▶ **A stationary car** could suggest you want to 'get a move on', or that you yearn for time away from the rat race – consider how you were feeling at this point in the dream.

▶ **Being the passenger** implies passivity and lack of control, most especially if you are in the back seat.

▶ **Involvement in an accident** may be your subconscious telling you to slow down in life.

▶ **Having your car stolen** relates to a loss of identity, which is perhaps from a failed relationship or job.

▶ **Pulling up into a driveway** shows that you have found security at the end of your journey.

Flying

Flying is one of the most common dreams – see box, right. You may not be surprised to learn that Freud associated flying with sexual desire. Modern Freudians link the act of throwing yourself off a cliff in a hang glider with sexual exhilaration. However, other people interpret flying dreams as a kind of 'out of body' experience.

▶ **A sense of fear when flying** suggests anxiety about being able to rise to the challenges in your life.

▶ **Flying in a glider** shows you 'going with the flow' rather than taking the initiative.

Lorry

These vehicles carry similar meanings to cars, but, of course, they are used to carry large loads commercially, so there may be different implications. You may be feeling overloaded or be finding it difficult to get going. The lorry represents how easy or hard you are finding it to get things moving.

good to know

Flying through history
People have always dreamed of flying, and the subject remains of enduring interest around the globe (there is even a website dedicated to it: www.members.aol.com/caseyflyer/flying/dreams):

▶ Flying was often seen as a good omen, for example Artemidorus (see page 22), provided that the dreamer landed easily. He believed flying indicated skill at business, and the greater the height achieved, the more prosperity was to come.

▶ In Africa and the Pacific islands, flying denoted success and long life.

▶ In tenth-century Baghdad, Mas'udi Ali ibn Husayn expressed the view that flying dreams revealed the travels of the soul. The Native American Tachini concur, believing that our spirit flies with other spirits when we dream, returning with messages from the dead.

Motorbike

Motorbikes combine the ideas of sexuality, power and youth. So travelling on a motorbike symbolizes sexual drive, energy, adventure and a sense of restlessness.

Road

Roads symbolize where you see yourself going in your life. This could be on an emotional, spiritual or practical level. New directions signify the pursuit of new goals. Major roads such as motorways are more significant than small, inconsequential roads. Anything appearing on or by the road has a meaning related to your current aims. Consider how you were driving – recklessly, against the flow of traffic, breaking a rule?

▶ **A difficult, winding or bumpy road** suggests that you feel there are obstacles holding up your progress.

▶ **A dark road** indicates unknown, possibly frightening events to come.

▶ **A straight road** implies smooth progress, especially if the borders are green.

▶ **Road signs** will carry symbolic meaning.

▶ **Crossroads or forks in the road** indicate choices, or opposing views.

▶ **One-way roads** show you feel you have no way of going back.

▶ **Roadblocks** are major obstacles in your chosen path.

Subway

Any underground location reveals the subconscious at work. Subways need careful consideration because people who use them all the time regard them as familiar, while others regard them as threatening and alien. If you don't use subways regularly, treat it as a message about your inner self. Consider the rest of the dream to decide if your subconscious is here concerned with emotions, sexuality or some insight into your waking life.

Time travel
This suggests a desperate wish to escape from reality. Consider where you jumped to in time – it could be part of your life when you were happier.

Train
Like all journeys, train rides show your path through life, or an aspect of it. Trains follow tracks, so they can represent conformity (or a need for it) in your life. If you feel 'on the right track', you are comfortable with the direction your life is taking. Of course, we also choose which train to take, so consider if you did this in your dream, and what the other trains may represent. Freud believed that the usual meaning of a train was sexual.

▶ **Moving along the train** shows you visiting the different compartments of your life.
▶ **Missing a train** suggests missing an important opportunity, perhaps by being hesitant.
▶ **Freight trains** carry the burdens of life.
▶ **Train stations** are points at which you make choices about where you are going, so are powerfully symbolic.

did you know?

Einstein and the sled
Scientist Alfred Einstein said that as a boy he dreamt of a nighttime sled ride when he zoomed at great speed down a hillside. When he was moving as fast as light, the stars in the sky became distorted and their patterns changed. Many years later the dream was part of the inspiration for his theory of relativity.

Water

Water is an important symbol in dreams. As a basic life need, it represents life itself (and therefore death), but it is also closely identified with our emotions and our ability to deal with them. To Freud, water was the womb: protected, dependent on the mother. To Christians, it symbolizes renewal (through baptism).

must know

Water in dreams
► The meaning for the dreamer will be partly dependent on how they view water, whether they feel comfortable in and on it, and whether it brings images of relaxation or threat.
► However, it is such a basic element of life that water has resonances in our inner psyche.
► Clear, calm waters suggest serenity and being in touch with yourself.
► Troubled waters suggest just that: trouble through not being able to control or express your feelings or accept those of others.

Beach See page 165.

Boat
Vessels such as a boat or ship travel across water, so they represent our emotional journey. The condition of the boat indicates how well you cope with and express your feelings. Where you are on the boat shows your ability to control these sentiments: if you are at the helm, you are in charge. Of course, the thing about boats is that you can't get off, so the journey you are on has many obligations and restrictions that you have to work with. Jumping off the boat indicates your unwillingness to do this. The state of the sea tells you more about your emotional life (see Sea). Freud saw ships as phallic symbols, suggesting that the size of the boat grew to match the preoccupation with sex. So a ship struggling through rough seas depicts the dreamer's sexual uncertainty.

Floating
► **If you are floating on water,** you are 'going with the flow' – accepting what is happening without intervening, perhaps because you are trying to avoid responsibility.

▶ **If you feel comfortable,** you are quite happy to let others set the emotional pace.

▶ **If you feel trapped** but unable to do anything about it, there is a suggestion of self-doubt and over-reliance on others to pull you through. You may be feeling confused about where you are going in a relationship.

Flood

A flood suggests being overwhelmed by emotions that were previously repressed. Being swept away by a flood indicates your lack of control of, or comprehension of, these feelings and indicates depression. More positively, many creation stories use floods as devices to get rid of bad things and initiate new life, so the flood represents new energy. This interpretation fits in with Freud's view of water as representing the womb.

Fountain

A fountain pushes water up in a pleasing way – so fountains represent freedom to express emotion, and a sense of joy. This suggests happiness in a (new?) relationship.

Harbour

Harbours are places of refuge from dangerous seas, so in a dream a harbour is where you seek shelter from a difficult situation, such as a stormy relationship. It is also, like a quay, a place from where new journeys can begin. So you are picturing a calm, reflective space from where you can start again. The more ships there are at the quayside, the more opportunities you have.

must know

Boating facts
▶ **Small boats** such as rowboats or canoes take much more physical effort to move, indicating the effort required to show your emotions.
▶ **Ferries** show transition, as they transfer you from one part of your world to another, often between relationships.
▶ **Getting off a boat** suggests a new phase in your life – are you alone or accompanied?
▶ **A night sea journey** is a voyage into your unconscious, to your very roots.
▶ **A boat capsizing** indicates inability to cope with emotions.

Ice

Ice is frozen water, so can symbolize blocked emotions and lack of progress – being cold, even frigid, in relationships. It is also risky to walk on, so there is a sense of fear and caution about something.

▶ **Falling through the ice** suggests that your feelings are about to crash into your consciousness.

▶ **An icicle is a frozen phallic symbol**, which indicates blocked male sexual feelings.

Lake or lagoon

These are generally calm, relaxed places, suggesting spiritual or emotional enlightenment. For interpretation, much depends on the surroundings: are they mountainous (obstacles) or verdant forest (where the imagination flourishes)? Consider the water. Clear water suggests peace and happiness, lack of complications. Murky water indicates less clarity in thought and expression, difficulty in relationships.

▶ **Wading or swimming** in the water suggests spiritual peace and calm.

▶ **Sinking into the lake** indicates introversion.

▶ **Choppy, stormy waters** indicate a troubled relationship.

▶ **Drowning in water** represents lack of control over your feelings, particularly expressing them.

Marsh

As with other unreliable surfaces, this shows emotional instability, and a feeling of being bogged down, and unable to meet your responsibilities.

Pond

A pond is a way of containing water, suggesting that you are keeping your own feelings in check, and perhaps not acknowledging their depth. The pond may represent a desire for emotional calm and control.

Rain

Rain brings growth as it fertilizes the ground. It is a sign that you are coming to terms with a problem, maybe with the help of your imagination (because rain is water that comes through the air). There are associations with spiritual growth through rain, through its cleansing qualities.

River

Rivers carry all the symbolism of water, but there is an extra element because they flow on a journey, which has parallels with our lives: starting very small, meandering between experiences until eventually reaching an end when we are no more. So rivers can symbolize our own life process, reflecting the changes in our bodies, our moods and the events in our lives. Thus a full-flowing river suggests vitality, and a dried up or stagnant one indicates low energy.

▶ **Crossing rivers** indicates change.

▶ **Seeing others cross rivers** reveals thoughts of mortality.

▶ **Travelling upstream** suggests working against our own feelings.

Sea

The sea is a powerful, mysterious force capable of bringing and taking life. As such, it can be taken as a symbol for life, cosmic consciousness, or, to some interpreters, motherhood. Since water has emotional significance, the massive scale of seas and oceans suggests that they represent vast, limitless feelings – emotions that can overwhelm. Consider the state of the waters: clear or murky? Calm or troubled? Your feelings towards the sea will influence your dreams, too, depending on whether you admire its beauty or fear its power. Since we do not live in the sea, it can also represent somewhere where we cannot survive: a challenging environment.

Snow

Snow represents feelings that have been repressed, or at least not expressed, for a long time, suggesting inhibitions and a lack of emotional response. You may be isolated from others, perhaps by fear or some other obstacle.

▶ **Clean white snow** suggests innocence and a new start.

▶ **Dirty snow** reveals feelings of guilt and feeling tainted.

▶ **Playing in the snow** implies a wish to return to the innocence and fun of childhood.

Swimming

When we swim, we control our passage through water, so on a symbolic level we are in charge of our emotional life and expression. There is also the idea of exploration and survival, and it is worth recalling what you were swimming towards or from, just as in life we 'sink or swim' when faced with difficulties on our own. Swimming can symbolize a period of transition, such as adolescence, or a change of environment. You can deduce further meanings depending on how you were swimming:

▶ **Against the tide:** Encountering opposition.
▶ **Underwater:** Being aware of your subconscious.
▶ **Easily:** Coping well with relationships.
▶ **With others:** Feeling connected in society.

Swimming pool

This combines the symbolism of water with a social situation. Consider who else is by the pool, and how you are interacting with them in your dream. Are you on the outside, looking on enviously at the lives of others? Are you part of the group, fitting in well?

Tap

Strange as it may seem, taps have an important symbolic role because we use them to control water, or our emotions.

▶ **A leaky tap** indicates difficulty in handling or expressing your feelings.
▶ **Someone else working the tap** suggests the dreamer feels controlled in a relationship, and is not able to communicate this message.

Underwater

There are a number of interpretations for being underwater in a dream. An underwater location can indicate a need for a slower, calmer life where you feel more in touch with your own feelings. This is far from land, suggesting a desire to get away from everyday life and problems. However, since water is a major symbol for emotions, being immersed in it can also indicate that you are overwhelmed by your feelings, unable to rationalize about things. Being surrounded by fluid can also represent a return to the womb, where you feel safe but are helpless. Consider the context of the whole dream to decide which interpretation makes most sense for you.

Water

Water in your dream symbolizes your unconscious and emotional state of mind. It has associations with spirituality, energy and nourishment, but also with danger and strange environments. Water as a positive symbol suggests a new life, cleansing and purity. It also shows our capacity for different emotions – water has no shape. Positive symbols apply when the dreamer controls the water, or feels in control in it. However, there are negative image associations too. These indicate feelings of being overwhelmed or repressed and fears about being out of control or far from support.

▶ **Calm, clear water** indicates purity and a sense of wellbeing.
▶ **Entering water** suggests new feelings, perhaps sexual.
▶ **Dirty, murky water** indicates negative or unexpressed feelings.
▶ **Deep water** suggests uncertainty.
▶ **Boiling water** indicates emotional turmoil.

Waterfall

A waterfall unleashes an unstoppable torrent of water. In dreams, water represents emotions, so a waterfall is a massive release of feelings that have been pent up for a long time and now cannot be stopped.

▶ **If you are watching the waterfall,** you are looking at a flow of repressed emotion.
▶ **If you are under the waterfall,** all those feelings will land on you, so much so that it could be a threat.

Waves

Waves are movement of water, representing how your emotions are being expressed and what your impulses are. Calm, regular waves indicate emotional control and a love of the sensuous. Being caught in a tidal wave suggests you are being pulled along by (possibly sexual) feelings that you are unable to control. Surfing a wave means you are riding a range of emotions, indicating confidence in your own feelings.

Websites

Sites about sleep and dreams
http://science.howstuffworks.com/dream.htm (studies the nature of dreams and dream theories)
http://sommeil.univ-lyon1.fr/articles/listes/en/jouvet.html (links to various articles about sleep)
www.aasmnet.org (website of the American Academy of Sleep Medicine)
www.dreams.ca/science.htm (dream research and sleep disorders)
www.esrs.org (website of the European Sleep research Society)
www.fireflysun.com/book/ (has a section discussing the nature of dreams)
www.lboro.ac.uk/departments/hu/groups/sleep/index.htm (Loughborough Sleep Research Centre)
www.oniros.fr/assoceasd (website of the European Association for the Study of Dreams)
www.rationality.net/why.htm (has a section on why and how we sleep)l

Other perspectives
http://library.thinkquest.org/11189/nfhistory.htm (history of dream interpreting)
http://people.uncw.edu/deagona/ancientnovel/diana.htm (the history of ancient Greek dream interpretation)
http://samvak.tripod.com/dream.html (about divination through dreams)
http://veda.harekrsna.cz/encyclopedia/dreams.htm (gives a Hindu perspective on dreaming)
www.acadine.org/w/Main_Page (has a section on dreaming, including a 1916 view of dreaming premonitions)
www.dreamanalysis.info/ (a site dedicated to the understanding and exploration of dreams, especially the Jungian and archetypal school of dream analysis)
www.geocities.com/sellonge (a pilot study about the idea that dreams go over feelings the dreamer experienced in recent life)
www.iranian.com/Iranica/Sept97/Dream/index.html (gives an insight in to pre- and post-Islamic Persian dream interpretation)
www.isidore-of-seville.com/astdiv/3.html (numerous links to sites covering the history of dream interpretation)
www.newadvent.org/cathen/05154a.htm (gives a Catholic perspective on dreams)

Lucid dreaming
www.lucid.tv/ (devoted to lucid dreaming)
www.lucidity.com (all about lucid dreaming)
www.spiralnature.com/magick/dreams/awakeinsleep.html (how to become a lucid dreamer)

Dream interpretation
www.dreamgate.com/dream/resources/online_a.htm (links to many sites about dreaming)
www.dreamhawk.com (the website of prolific author on this subject, Tony Crisp)
www.dreammoods.com/ (gives interpretations for many types of dream)
www.experiencefestival.com/dreams (a general resource site on dreams)

www.humanform.info/htm/dreams.htm (looks at dream imagery and interpretation)
www.psy.pdx.edu/PsiCafe/Areas/ParanormalPsy/Dreams.htm (has links to many dream analysis sites)

Online dream dictionaries

http://ibs.howstuffworks.com/ibs/den/dream10.htm
http://predictions.astrology.com/dd/category.html
www.crystalinks.com/dreams.html
www.dreamloverinc.com/dictionary1.htm
www.dreamsleep.net
www.hyperdictionary.com/dream
www.ivillage.co.uk/astrology/dreamdictionary/list/category
www.maljonicsdreams.com
www.newagedirectory.com/dream/dictionary.htm
www.petrix.com/dreams/
www.sleeps.com/dictionary/dictionary.html
www.swoon.com/dream/

Discussion sites

www.aboutmydream.com/forums/
www.dreamviews.com/

Books

Jack Altman, *1001 Dreams* (Duncan Baird Publishers)
Pamela Ball, *The Complete Dream Dictionary* (Chartwell Books)
The Classic 1000 Dreams (Foulsham)
Tony Crisp, *Dream Dictionary* (Dell) (one of many books by this author)
Peter and Elizabeth Fenwick, *The Hidden Door: Understanding and Controlling Dreams* (Berkeley Publishing)
Sigmund Freud, *The Interpretation of Dreams* (Wordsworth and Penguin)
Dan Gollub, *Interpreting and Understanding Dreams* (Nova Science Publishers)
Soozi Holbeche, *Dreams* (Thorsons)
C. G. Jung, *Memories, Dreams, Reflections* (Fontana)
Mehr-ali Kalami, *The New Dream Interpreter* (Quantum)
Stephen LaBerge, Howard Rheingold, *Exploring the World of Lucid Dreaming* (Ballantine Books)
Lisa Lenard, *Guide to Dreams* (Dorling Kindersley)
Caro Ness, *Secrets of Dreams* (Dorling Kindersley)
Marci Pliskin, *The Complete Idiot's Guide to Interpreting Your Dreams* (Alpha)
David Shulman (ed.), *Dream Cultures* (OUP)
Anthony Stevens, *Jung: A very short introduction* (Oxford Books)

Glossary

Amplification: The process developed by Carl Jung to investigate dream meaning by exploring any of its archetypes, mythology and connections to the dreamer's psychology and life.

Anima: The psyche's female personality traits (see also page 156).

Animus: The psyche's male personality traits (see also page 156).

Archetype: Symbolic image derived from our collective experience and present in the individual unconscious. These 'mythological motifs', as Carl Jung dubbed them, appear repeatedly in stories, myths and dreams. Examples include the Great Mother (see page 158) and the Old Man (see page 160).

Aromatherapy: Relaxing fragrances from essential oils and herbs that can aid sleep and dreaming.

Bruxism: Grinding teeth while asleep.

Collective unconscious: The universal symbolism found in myths from many cultures – the aspects of the psyche shared by everyone. The concept originated from Carl Jung.

Dream catcher: A web-like device that is made by North Americans and which traps bad dreams.

Dream group: A group of people who discuss each other's dreams as an aid to interpretation.

Dream persona: The person representing you in your dream, who may be you, or a changed version of you, or someone whose characteristics represent you.

Ego: The conscious 'I' or 'me' of the psyche that experiences the external world (see also page 27).

Extrasensory perception: *See* Paranomal dreams.

Free association: An open way of talking or thinking that follows and reveals (often unconscious) links between ideas.

Freud, Sigmund (1856–1939): Austrian psychoanalyst who studied dreams and believed they could be interpreted to explain the dreamer's secret desires. He was a strong believer that dreams often originated from sexual feelings (see also page 26–7).

Gestalt: The German word for 'form' or 'shape' and describes a technique developed by Fritz Perls (1893–1970). In Gestalt therapy, the dreamer considers the meaning and implications of their own dream, without interpretation from an analyst. It aims to build independence through self-knowledge.

Hypnogogia: The term for hallucinations and visions seen just before you fall asleep. The images are often vividly coloured.

Hypnopompia: Visions seen just before waking.

Id: The part of the psyche concerned with pleasure, encouraging you to follow your desires (see also page 27).

Incubation: An age-old practice of inducing sleep in order to dream, often in the hope of receiving healing or advice.

Jung, Carl (1875–1961): Swiss psycholanalyst who studied under Freud and developed the idea that dreams involve the collective unconscious (see also page 28).

Lucid dreaming: Knowing you are dreaming during a dream. Also known as conscious dreaming.

Night terrors: Partial awakening provoked by disturbing dreams during a deep sleep cycle, often resulting in a raised heartbeat and perspiring.
Nightmare: A highly disturbing dream that induces such great fear and anxiety that you wake up.
Nocturnal emission: Male ejaculation during sleep, also called a 'wet dream', most common in the teenage years. Often, but not always, linked to erotic dreams.

Oneiromancy: The practice of divinition by dream interpretation.
Oneirology: The scientific discipline of dream research.
Out of body experience (OBE): The feeling that you are separated from your physical body, often linked with near-death experiences.

Paranormal dreams: Psychic dreams, which some argue are the result of extrasensory perception (ESP) and seem to contain information not available elsewhere. Examples include telepathic dreams, when we receive dream images from others; clairvoyant dreams, in which the dreamer receives information about an object; and precognitive dreams (see below).

Parasomnia: The group term for sleep disorders, such as sleep walking and night terrors (see also page 33).
Persona: The 'face' that we show to the exterior world.
Precognitive dream: A dream in which you experience a future event.
Prodromal dream: A controversial idea that a dream can indicate a disease you may be suffering from.
Psyche: The collective term for both our conscious and unconscious mental processes – the human mind (the word is the Greek for 'soul').

Rapid eye movement (REM): Our most vivid (and therefore memorable) dreams happen during the REM sleep phase, which is part of our sleep cycle. Although the eyes move, the body is held in a state near paralysis (see also page 32). REM is also known as paradoxical sleep.
Repression: The process of excluding memories and impulses that we are not comfortable with. The memories can, however, be freed up in the unconscious mind during dreams.
Reverse learning theory: The idea that dreams are the brain's way of disposing of unwanted information.

Shadow: The personality traits repressed by our superego in our unconscious because they do not fit with our persona.
Subconscious: The level just below consciousness.
Superego: The conscience that enforces moral codes and reflects parental influence, restraining the demands of the id.

Index

Index

☼ Collins need to know?

Look out for these recent titles in Collins' practical and accessible
need to know? series.

Other titles in the series:

**To order any of these titles,
please telephone 0870 787 1732
quoting reference 263H.**
For further information about all
Collins books, visit our website:
www.collins.co.uk